CW00970111

Cézanne

Nils Peters

Jean Prouvé

1901–1984

The Dynamics of Creation

TASCHEN

HONG KONG KÖLN LONDON LOS ANGELES MADRID PARIS TOKYO

Photo page 2 ► Jean Prouvé in his private house, 1955
Illustration page 4 ► C.I.M.T. façade-panels for schools, perspective view, 1962

© 2006 TASCHEN GmbH
Hohenzollernring 53, D-50672 Köln
www.taschen.com
© 2006 VG Bild-Kunst, Bonn, for the works of Jean Prouvé

Editor ► Peter Gössel, Bremen
Design and layout ► Gössel und Partner, Bremen
Project management ► Katrin Schumann, Eike Meyer, Bremen
Text edited by ► Johannes Althoff, Hélène Pieper, Berlin
Translation ► Karl Edward Johnson, Berlin

Printed in Germany
ISBN-13: 978-3-8228-4878-4
ISBN-10: 3-8228-4878-6

To stay informed about upcoming TASCHEN titles, please request our magazine at www.taschen.com/magazine or write to TASCHEN America, 6671 Sunset Boulevard, Suite 1508, USA-Los Angeles, CA 90028, contact-us@taschen.com, Fax: +1-323-463.4442. We will be happy to send you a free copy of our magazine which is filled with information about all of our books.

Contents

6 Introduction

18 Entrance Portal Villa Reifenberg
19 Furniture for the Cité Universitaire in Nancy
22 Standard Chair
24 Aero Club Roland Garros
26 Maison du Peuple
30 Classroom Table with Two Chairs
32 Garden Furniture for the U.A.M. Pavilion
34 Demountable Barrack Units
35 Maisons à Portiques
38 Meridian Hall
40 "Guéridon" Table
42 Standard Houses
46 Houses for the Tropics
48 School in Vantoux
50 Grand Palais of the Lille Fairgrounds
52 Shed Roofs for the Mame Printing Works
54 Maisons Coques
58 Lecture Hall Chair
60 "Compas" Table System
62 Prouvé Residence
66 Façade of the Apartment Building on Mozart Square
68 Pavilion for the centennial of Aluminum
72 "Antony" Chair
74 House for Abbé Pierre
76 Cachat Pump-Room in Evian
78 Temporary School Building in Villejuif
80 Seynave Vacation House
82 Gauthier House
84 Youth Center in Ermont
86 Tour Nobel
88 Grid Frame Constructions

92 Life and Work
96 Bibliography / Credits

Introduction

Prouvé in a glider constructed by one of his trainees, 1936

For a long period of time the lifework of artistic blacksmith, designer, and manufacturer Jean Prouvé seemed either misunderstood or forgotten. However, in recent years his work attracted again the interest of both the architectural world and a broader public. Compared with other works regarded today as architectural icons of the Modern, Prouvé's creations are harder to understand and categorize in their proper context. This has much to do with the fact that he left behind a complex and diverse oeuvre of objects meant for everyday use, ranging from furniture designs, façades to complete houses. Justifiably architects such as Renzo Piano and Norman Foster refer to him as someone who intelligently connected a material's capability to an aesthetic born of a construction's logic, and who, while doing so, created a manifesto of early high-tech architecture.

It should nevertheless be kept in mind that this man, whose intensely professional and personal exchange included some of the best-known architects of his days, among them Le Corbusier, Frank Lloyd Wright, and Oscar Niemeyer, never actually studied architecture. Hence, Prouvé never was granted registration as an architect. In that respect, his architectural work seems best understood as shining through the works of other constructional artists, who he collaborated with or supported on an advisory level. Yet not only in the artistic realm Prouvé participated in the radical changes of his day; he also forged new paths as an employer, introducing teamwork, employees' participation in the design of the work process, as well as in finding answers to social questions.

Jean Prouvé was an untiring creator, permanently driven by hunger for knowledge. With great seriousness he dedicated himself to exploring the very essence of matter, and he unceasingly encouraged its development—at times even impetuously. He perceived the accomplishments in the technical field (to which he also contributed) with an almost childlike enthusiasm. During his 1964 lecture, held on the occasion of an exhibition of French industrial products in Warsaw, his words of praise for the technical achievements of his day were hymn-like: "How splendid they are—our space rockets and aircrafts, our cars and bicycles, our motorcycles, trains, machines, dams, and bridges, our small sailing vessels, and all the rest! Need I go on? The list is long enough to show us that so much scientific and industrial output is simply thrilling. Hardly any more words seem necessary—this tremendous situation speaks for itself." When considering Prouvé's complete oeuvre, we must keep in mind his almost effusive attitude, supported by his belief in a better world. It is a key to his personality and to an era of boundless belief in progress—the days when just about everything seemed possible.

Born April 8, 1901, Jean Prouvé was raised in a family of artists with strong ties to the crafts traditions in its hometown of Nancy. His father, Victor Prouvé, son of a painter who decorated faience earthenware, was an artisan and painter himself. His mother was the pianist Marie Duhamel, whose musical nature prompted Prouvé to say of his childhood: "I grew up in a music box."

Left page:
Staircase of the Institut Français des Pétroles

Prouvé as an apprentice in Émile Robert's workshop

In the early 1900s Nancy was a center for the blacksmith's trade and steel industry, but also well-known as a center for the crafts trade, especially for manufacturing furniture and glass. Together with Prouvé's godfather, Émile Gallé, Victor Prouvé co-founded the "School of Nancy," a grouping together of various Art Nouveau artists, artisans, and manufacturers, among which were the Daum brothers, who worked artistically with glass, and the artistic carpenter Louis Majorelle. The association opposed historicism, striving—just as the Arts and Crafts Movement of that time—not only for a revival of the fine arts, but also for a suffusing of everyday life with the arts, accompanied by a re-established union of life and art. As early influences, all of this contributed to Prouvé's progressive attitude, to his willingness to explore every new development, to his inclination to make industrial products available to everyone, to his way of approaching the whole of a matter, and to one of his greatest maxims: never devote one's own creativity to a copy.

Prouvé said once: "I developed a facility for the blacksmith's trade at the age of ten. It showed itself in a passion for machinery, which even then drove me to build things—something that has remained an undying and self-revitalizing passion of mine ever since. There might be a house to build in the garden—to be lived in, of course—or a car with special steering and brakes and with an engine yet to come. In the mind and actions of a child, all these things presupposed the urge to forge steel, to shape and adjust it, to unite it with wood; to rivet and regulate objects, and to simply make things run. For me, all this developed in stages along with my passion for aviation, which was still in its infancy at that time."

Prouvé's childhood dream of studying engineering would never come true. On a financial level the outbreak of World War I struck his family hard, and his father had difficulties finding commissions at all. In 1916 the father sent his son to train for three years with a friend, the artistic blacksmith Émile Robert, who lived in Enghien on the outskirts of Paris. In Prouvé's own words, this was how he came to spend his earliest years of apprenticeship "at the forge". For his further training Prouvé chose to study under the Hungarian artistic blacksmith Adalbert Szabo, back then one of the leading artisans. Through Szabo, who also worked for different architectural offices, Prouvé for the first time came in contact with the constructing arts. Following his military service from 1921–1923 (he served in the Calvary), another of his father's friends, anthropologist Saint-Just Péquart, gave Prouvé the financial support allowing him to open his own workshop for the artistic blacksmith trade. In early 1924 Prouvé moved into 300 square yards of work space located at 35 Rue du Géneral Custine in Nancy. The very same year he married painter Madeleine Schott, one of his father's students.

Initially Prouvé began by producing cast-iron lamps, iron handrails, and gates, whose ornamentation revealed a strong Art Nouveau influence. Not much later, influenced by modernism, he turned his attention to far more daring forms, developing an interest in new materials. This automatically called for acquiring newer tools and machines. In 1926 he came to experiment with stainless steel, at that time a new material, which he handled using the most modern of welding machinery. It was also during this period that Prouvé first confronted avant-garde architecture. His professional breakthrough came in 1927, when he received the commission to design an interior entranceway for Reifenberg's city villa in Paris from the architect Robert Mallet-Stevens, one of the leading French representatives of the modern building arts. This opened his way into the circle around Le Corbusier, the outstanding French avant-garde architect.

Official opening of the street "Rue Mallet-Stevens" on July 20, 1927, in Paris. Prouvé appears in the picture on the right.

Over the following years Prouvé created his first pieces of furniture such as chairs and tables, soon to be followed by windows, movable wall elements made of steel paneling, elevator cabins, doors (his first patent on sheet-metal doors was filed in 1929). Undeniable by now was that more than simply a shift in his areas of activity had come about; there was also the steady growth of his business. By the late 1920s Prouvé employed nearly 30 co-workers. In 1931, due to drastically increased commissions and newly acquired machinery, the production was relocated to a building on Rue des Jardiniers, and the firm restructured to form a stock corporation, called the "Sociéte Anonyme Les Ateliers Jean Prouvé".

In 1930, together with Mallet-Stevens, Charlotte Perriand, Le Corbusier, Pierre Jeanneret, Marcel Lods, Eugène Beaudouin and Tony Garnier, Prouvé was among the co-founders of the "Union des Artistes Modernes" (U.A.M.), an amalgamation of architects and designers dedicated to establishing a connection between art and industrial production. When he presented the first of his furniture and door designs at the shows organized by the U.A.M., the character of his future work was already recognizable in these exhibits: technical objects, so well thought-out in every detail and so clearly fabricated that nothing about them was concealed: the actual construction functioned as the all-defining design element.

Prouvé once described the "guidelines" of his work as follows: "...partly by following the evolution of science which governs the development of techniques, partly by accumulating information and studying materials and their treatment. Next, by watching work in operation. Further, by seeking inspiration and discovering the options available through the practice of advanced techniques. Finally, by never postponing decisions, so as neither to lose impetus nor indulge in unrealistic forecasts. I soon discovered that we come upon fulfillment and disappointment in the actual performing of a task, and not in mere words. Above all, one should not sketch out utopian projects, because evolution can only result from practical experience..." In his work Prouvé pursued everything but the creation of the monumental. His primary concern was the

notion of human beings living in a flexible and changeable modern environment. For him, this also meant that buildings, for example, had to be further developed, altered, and rethought, just like cars or aeroplanes. In this respect he criticized: "It's a fact that highly industrialized items, whether they fly or stand, exist in a state of perpetual development and even their prices are sinking. The only industry that fails to function this way is the construction industry."

Although the constant optimizing and simplifying of the production process was essential to a product's development, it generated at the same time a certain unpredictability. In 1989, a former manager at the Prouvé workshops recalled: "It was hard working with him. He would give us a sketch, or some hurried plan he just drew up, and say: 'Make this!' And eight days later, after the work was finished and ready to be delivered, he would say: 'This has to be changed!'... It would have been better to just hide the plans—to finally get the work done."

Prouvé refused to work with materials in a way of which he thought that it veiled the construction process, calling it "hypocritical." He disapproved of the steel-tube aesthetic used by Marcel Breuer, the designer of the first steel-tube armchair, because the flow of energy through the employed material was virtually undetectable. By comparison, Prouvé's work was more the result of constant searching and improving, focused on combining a well-conceived comfort and wide variability with a rational production method. "If today's latest aircraft designs recall the most delicate of birds, this is simply because the means to build them in this fashion are now available. Voisin's first aircrafts, these chicken coops, could have never been constructed any other way at the beginning of the century, and yet Voisin was making as careful a study of birds as those made today." All his professional life, Prouvé refused to design for the sake of form alone. Moreover, the appearance of an object was always expected to reflect the process of its creation.

The success of the business was most of all based on its multitalented founder. Prouvé could draw, experiment, weld, find commissions, handle the deal-making—

"Grand repos" armchair, 1930

and, not least of all, run the business on a daily basis. Equally remarkable was the virtually perfect teamwork. Everyone involved worked together in a single space, so that every co-worker, whether a planner or metalwork technician, always knew the production's stage of development at any given moment. Characteristic of the general procedure was an almost "tactile" working method, which respected the progression from design to prototype, from adapting the prototype to completing production renderings, and then moved from the completed renderings to producing the finished object. The production's work stages were so carefully coordinated one with the other, and so intertwined, that it evoked the impression to be the labor of a single individual. For Prouvé, while keeping track of the smallest of details, production was founded on saving time, saving material, and saving on manual labor.

His best-known work of the 1930s is the exceptional "Maison du Peuple" (People's House), erected in Clichy from 1935–1939. The building, declared a national landmark in 1981, displays the full scope of its creator's ideas. Nearly all building parts are made of sheet metal: the flexible interior walls, lightweight staircases made of steel, and prefabricated ceilings. For the first time façade panels were used, a forerunner of the curtain wall façade, for which Prouvé is still considered the co-inventor. It was built around the same time as the equally revolutionary airfield pavilion near Versailles, the Aero Club "Roland Garros". Built to completion in Jean Prouvé's workshops, the construction was erected in only two weeks and its static connections were based on no more than simple bolted connections.

Design of a newspaper stand, 1935

In addition to constructing buildings the "Jean Prouvé Studios" were also contracted to produce large amounts of furniture for schools, offices, train stations, and universities. Another area of the studios' production concerned developing bicycles and trailers. During this period the workshops employed 47 workers and 14 additional office workers. The accumulated profits were invested in new machinery in order to keep up with competitors. At the same time the business allowed its employees paid vacations as well as additional insurance coverage—in other words, Prouvé realized what other employers only discussed.

Due to the scarcity of steel during the German occupation, the workshop shifted to working more with materials such as wood and aluminum. Conceived around this time were the demountable pavilions. The production line also included wooden carburetors for trucks, ovens, and sheet-steel bicycle frames. Prouvé actively participated with his workshops in resisting the German occupation by aiding the dismantling and re-working of the country's railway lines, for which he was elected Mayor of Nancy after the occupation period ended. But this affair with politics remained an intermezzo.

After the war the industrialist René Schwarz, a friend of the Prouvé family, helped in redesigning the business according to Prouvé's ideas. This resulted in new workshops being built in Maxéville, a suburb of Nancy, where the production of industrial items and the completion of entire houses could now be carried out in grand style. The relocation to the new factory buildings was completed in 1947. In order to optimize production, the workshops were equipped with the latest machinery. The logistics of the overall production were coordinated by creating different work teams made up of designers, architects, architecture students, and technicians. Work-processes were discussed in a team, earnings sensibly divided among the participants, and the profits invested in acquiring new machinery. The same conditions that existed in the workshops in Nancy applied here as well.

Bicycle trailer, 1941

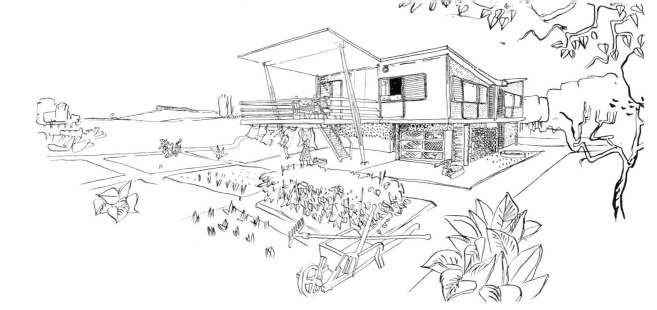

The Maxéville period marked the height of Jean Prouvé's productivity. The studios produced literally everything: banisters, kitchens, furniture, doors, windows, façades, wall and roof elements, as well as complete buildings. All of the studios' products were made in accordance with the same basic principle, to which Prouvé referred during his 1959 lecture in Brasilia: "Many things are built in the world at large: aircrafts, cars, machine tools, works of art, and much more. ... The individual or collective dwelling and the public building are objects constructed on a par with things such as these. ... Whenever an object needs to be made, there must always be a 'constructional concept' at the outset. One individual—namely the constructor or designer—suddenly sees it completed in three dimensions. He knows his materials—these materials also inspire him—and a choice has already been made. Whether the object is big or small, I'm convinced that whatever escapes this rule was never properly constructed." What Prouvé had formerly experimented with only as constructional forms, here in Maxéville now assumed a position in the forefront as basic structures and types in their own right. The static systems, presented partly by Prouvé himself in an "Alphabet of Structures," included building types with frames (portique), supporting cores (Alba), shell constructions (coque), so-called crutches (béquille), as well as vaulted structures (voûte). Later added to the structural palette in Maxéville were the stool-like structures known as "tabouret," and the grid frame constructions that enabled an unrestricted ground-floor plan.

This creative period not only brought about works that were revolutionary in the production field, but also in the area of assembly procedures for architectural objects on the whole—citing, for example, the apartment houses built in Meudon, the "Tropical Houses," and the building completed on Mozart Square in Paris. The workshops' furniture production was increased by winning competitions as well as through directly acquired commissions.

The workshops' pioneering spirit, together with its unconventional and successful track record, caught the attention of the aluminum industry, which offered tempting large-scale commissions and research money. In 1949, the Aluminium Français concern took part in the Jean Prouvé Studios with a capital sharing that would continually

Demountable house 26.2 x 26.2 feet, 1941
Pierre Jeanneret, architect

"Kangourou" armchair, 1948

increase over the following years. Only a few months later Prouvé signed a contract with Studal (Société Technique d'Utilisation d'Alliages Légers), a sister company of Aluminium Français that marketed its products, securing Studal the exclusive rights for the sale of the workshops' products. Increasingly Prouvé lost control over his own business. Misjudging the potential of the work concept, the new participants wasted no time restructuring the workshops.

In 1950 the Maxéville development office was shut down and relocated to Paris. This unhitched the development practices from the overall production and fairly torpedoed one of Prouvé's basic maxims. By 1952 Prouvé was denied access to his own workshops, and the department for manufacturing prototypes, once so important for him, was shut down as well. The following year, disappointed by the developments and with resignation, Jean Prouvé removed himself from the firm's directorship and would never again set foot on the grounds in Maxéville. Years later, recalling the separation from his own work, he summed up the break in just a few words: "I died in 1952."

"They have felled your timber, now make do with what's left," his friend, Le Corbusier, comforted him. Indeed, leaving the chair didn't only mean that Prouvé lost

House in Guerrevielle for the architect Raymond Lopez, 1953

Administration building and under-floor facilities of the EDF power station in Serre-Poncon (Hautes-Alpes), 1959

Gate to the machine rooms of the EDF dam's power station

his work, his workshops and staff but also the copyrights on his designs. However, he was able to keep names and the rights of use for more than 30 filed patents, ranging from his patents for inventions like the removable shed-roof, metal-door and window systems to the removable dividing walls and the metal-frame constructions of the "maisons à portiques."

During this transitional period, from 1954–1955, Prouvé briefly worked freelance for Aluminum Français. He produced the "Pavilion for the "Centennial of Aluminum", the long hoped-for residence of his own in Nancy, and the Institut Français des Pétroles. But collaborating with Aluminium Français was deeply unsatisfying. After taking the advice of a friend, writer and architect Michel Bataille, both Prouvé and Bataille founded in 1956 "Les Constructions Jean Prouvé" whose main office was located at 10 Rue Louvois in Paris.

With Paris now the professional nucleus of Prouvé's life, he was forced to commute between his Paris office and his private residence in Nancy, a situation that Prouvé—at heart a family man who loved company—found unbearable. One anecdote in connection with all his forced traveling even illuminates his love of company: on his way home from Paris, Prouvé regularly picked up hitchhikers in his sports car, and, whenever the stranger seemed stranded in the middle of the night, he offered the hitchhiker lodging—and so, on awakening the next morning, Prouvé's family often found complete strangers asleep in an armchair in the living room.

Unfortunately, even Prouvé's work for "Constructions Jean Prouvé" was strictly limited to designing. Although the unhitching of the practical applications from the overall

Saharan house on display at the Salon des Arts Ménagers, Paris, 1958
Arranged lengthwise are supports securing a shading roof made of a wood and aluminum sandwich element.

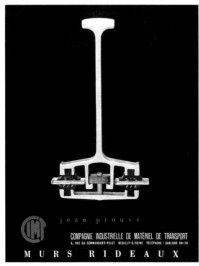

Posts of the curtain wall façade conceived by Prouvé, C.I.M.T., 1958
Advertisement from the magazine *L'Architecture d'aujourd'hui*, 1964

work process ran contrary to his basic convictions, this period nevertheless witnessed the planning and execution of magnificent buildings such as the "Cachat Pump-Room" in Évian, the interim school buildings (école nomade) erected in Villejuif, and the houses for the charity-minded benefactor and clergyman Abbé Pierre.

It was obvious that Prouvé was longing for the chance to involve himself again with assignments calling for more practical work. This chance seemed to show itself in 1957, when the concern Compagnie Industrielle de Matériel de Transport (C.I.M.T.), the maker of parts and accessories for railway lines—also the manufacturer of the sanitary cores for Abbé Pierre's Alba houses—decided to found and build a new Construction Department. The concern agreed to take over "Constructions Jean Prouvé" and make Jean Prouvé the department head. Under Prouvé's direction C.I.M.T. soon became the leading manufacturer of lightweight curtain wall façades. Now Prouvé worked on numerous façade solutions for large-scale projects such as the Músee du Harve and I.N.S.A. Institute in Lyon. But now, too, he had to accept being barred from integrating the design process into the overall production.

In the same year Prouvé received a chair of "Professionally Applied Arts" at the Conservatoire National des Arts et Métiers (C.N.A.M.), where his weekly lectures were always overcrowded. During these events Prouvé rarely said much. Instead, he made drawings and continually visualized his ideas on a chalkboard. What he illustrated here, true to his own convictions, was that the practice of theories was paramount and that any knowledge acquired only academically was hardly in the position to awaken creativity. This was not simply a conveying of information: it was his artistic credo.

Musée des Beaux-Arts André Malraux in Le Havre, 1960
André Malraux, Raymond Audigier and Guy Lagneau, architects

After leaving C.I.M.T in 1966 Prouvé founded another office, advising architects and firms on the transposing of their projects. This led to his collaborating with the architects Georges Candilis, Alexis Josic, and Shadrach Woods during the planning stages for the façade of a university building, nicknamed the "Rostlaube" (Rusted Pergola), on the campus of the Freie Universität in Berlin, and, with Jean de Mailly and Jacques Depussé, for the curtain wall façade of the Tour Nobel Building in the Paris suburb of La Défense. Together with structural engineer Léon Pétroff, he invented the flexibly-applied grid frame constructions, used for faculty buildings and gas stations, whose enormous load-bearing span enabled the creation of large and support-free spaces.

In 1971 Prouvé was greatly honored by being named chairman of the competition committee for the newly planned modern art museum in Paris, the Centre Georges Pompidou. The nomination and the competition commitee's final decision to have the museum built by the architectural team of Renzo Piano and Richard Rogers, polarized the architectural world: Prouvé, chairman of the competition, had no registration as an architect, heading a competition committee which stipulated that the commission for a national museum had to be awarded to non-French architects! Yet Prouvé's talents, beyond criticism, would have undoubtedly lent the perfect touch to this enormously unique design project, whose realization he contributed to.

In the 1970s and 1980s Prouvé received a great many national and international awards. Among others he was honored with the Netherlands Erasmus Prize for his life achievement. The laudatory speech summarized: "He devoted his life to integrating industry and architecture as a way to encourage the human aspects in our environment." There was no denying that Prouvé's guiding principles united his architectural creations with their surroundings, especially his objects, not only artistically and technically, but also socially Prouvé greatly surpassed a purely aesthetic-oriented application of modernism. He was by no means interested in merely the simple assembling of prefabricated building elements. What interested him most was exploring the depths of a given material, its expressive and economic possibilities, as well as its social significance. Therefore Jean Nouvel characterized Prouvé's work in brief: "Rarely that ethics have created such a clear beauty."

Yet not everyone found this form of beauty accessible. At that time, society was highly skeptical of the industrialized building method. Moreover, after the war, the lightweight building methods that Prouvé used for his buildings were not always appreciated by the French from the standpoint of their applied "poetics of construction". Often enough, they were associated with makeshift structures, and with accommodations for the poor. At that time as well, Prouvé's propagated reforms directed at conceiving an apartment—his progressive-minded dividing up of the ground-floor plan, for example, and the creation of a highly innovative and multifunctional living-room space (taken for granted nowadays)—were hard to put across, and sometimes met with great resistance. On the other hand, it does seems hard to avoid thinking that Prouvé sometimes underestimated the uniqueness of a building and the cultural value of architectural givens. There was the situation, for example, when he intended to build a demountable church with lightweight building materials; but the project was prematurely abandoned, because neither the necessary transportation capabilities nor the structure's conceptual lightness played a decisive role here. Many projects were, therefore, more at the mercy of Prouvé's strong-willed nature than they were their practicality or the hopes of having them built at all.

The economic and technical developments to come never confirmed Prouvé's ideas. On the contrary: as building materials, steel and aluminum were hardly integrated to the expected degree in building schemes. Ultimately, concrete, which was easier to apply, pushed metal out of the larger picture—along with the characteristic lightness of modern structures as unique as those created by Jean Prouvé.

Radar tower on the Island of Ouessant, France, 1980–1981
J.-M. Jacquin, architect

1927 ▸ Entrance Portal Villa Reifenberg

Paris ▸ Robert Mallet-Stevens, architect

Entrance portal of Reifenberg's city villa
View from inside the building

In 1927 Prouvé mustered up all his courage, visited the enormously busy architect Robert Mallet-Stevens without making an appointment, and showed him a portfolio of his work. After no more than a ten-minute conversation, he not only received the commission to design the entrance portal of the villa belonging to the pianist Reifenberg, Mallet-Stevens gave him the freedom to work as he pleased: "Don't worry about a drawing or cost estimate, just make me a grill!" stipulated the architect, who gave the young man only a month to plan and carry out the entire assignment.

When Mallet-Stevens saw the completed entrance portal, he was thrilled. Indeed Prouvé had created a well-crafted masterpiece, whose visual finesse first revealed itself through the viewer's movements: he glazed the band-steel elements with a clear varnish and fitted them together in a way that made the interior entrance portal appear transparent and permeable when viewed frontally; but when viewed from an angle, the entrance portal's grill appeared closed and impermeable, and so it functioned like a veil. Its appearance lent the villa a visually striking focal point. The notion of a changing transparency was a popular design theme of the early modern age, and Prouvé intuitively took hold of this motif and put it to use in his own interpretation.

Prouvé's first modern work, designed and executed at the age of 26, would open the doors for him to exclusive circles of French architects of the avant-garde.

1931 ▸ Furniture for the Cité Universitaire in Nancy

Model room at the Cité Universitaire with
Prouvé's furniture

Below:
Design sketches

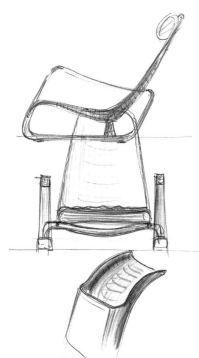

The furniture was created on the occasion of a competition for a new student dormitory at the Cité Universitaire in Nancy. With his workshops, Prouvé emerged as one of the competition's four winners and could design a quarter of the dormitory's furnishings. Yet compared with the designs of the other three first-prize winners, it was evident that only Prouvé's furniture could permanently satisfy the demands.

Prouvé's task included the design of beds, desks, bookshelves, armchairs, and standard chairs. As many as sixty pieces were produced of each object. For the first time he used wood as a building material (as a seating surface, for example). The supporting elements were bent C-shaped sections of sheet steel; in later works, sections of piping were used. All the furniture was conceived to require the least possible material expenditure during the production phase, which applied to the elegant armchair in particular. This made it possible to produce furniture both light and inexpensive to manufacture without forfeiting robustness. Elaborate mechanics were avoided. The armrests could be adjusted using simple leather straps with belt fasteners.

The seat of the armchair lies relatively low. After completing its first prototypes, a few of the older employees told their boss that it cost them a slight effort to raise themselves out of the armchair again. But Prouvé countered with: "It doesn't matter if you can't get out of it. It's designed for young people!" This timeless armchair is still in production today.

View of a room

Below:
Work table with chair

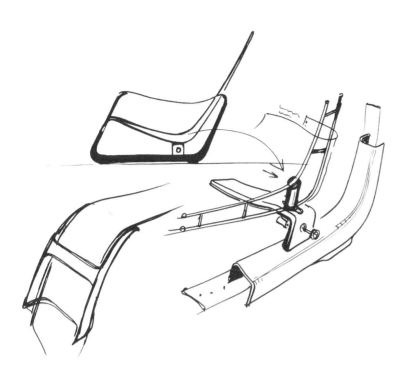

Left:
System sketches of the "Cité" armchair

Right:
The shelf belonging to the system

Profile of the "Cité" armchair

1934 ▸ Standard Chair

Two variations on the standard chair

This standard chair—following two folding chairs and the fourth chair in the series created in Prouvé's studio for the Cité Universitaire—was one of the most successful pieces of furniture to emerge from the Prouvé workshops, and its numerous variations were produced far into the 1950s. The forerunners of this model were two office chairs produced before 1934: the first, designed for the offices of the Electric Power Company in Paris, still featured armrests; the second strongly resembled the final model but was of slightly different proportions.

The Standard Chair is often compared to the cantilever chairs of the classical modern age because this clearly emphasizes Prouvé's different approach: he refuses all formalism and allows for the creation of form through the course of used energies. The

Serial production of the standard chair in
Prouvé's workshops

Below:
Design rendering, circa 1934

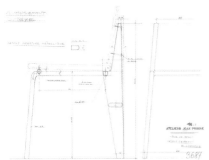

chair's back legs, which support the bulk of the weight, are made conspicuously massive. And Prouvé commented on this by saying that he intended to make visible "what the material thinks". Yet regarding the construction, critics accused him of over-exaggerating. This was not completely undeniable: Prouvé made sure that the chair could withstand up to 400 kg of weight.

1935–1936 ▸ Aero Club Roland Garros
Buc ▸ Eugène Beaudouin and Marcel Lods, architects

Left page:
Aerial view of the Aero Club in Buc

Above left:
Reduction of bolted connections for principal support elements

Above right:
Sheet-metal panels form the rear of the building

Design rendering, perspective drawing

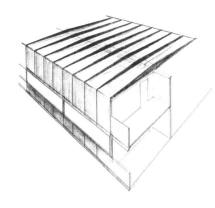

Prouvé received the commission for the Aero Club, near Versailles, from architect Marcel Lods, who settled a contract directly with the club's founders. Prouvé was given only a rough sketch from which to develop the details for a two-storey building as quickly as possible. During the work process, he produced sections of the building as prototypes and presented them to the architect. Lods, who originally planned to erect the building using a prefabricated, concrete construction method, changed his mind on the spot after seeing Prouvé's lightweight building parts and decided in favor of this other method.

The supporting framework consisted of welted sections of sheet metal, each no thicker than 4 mm and joined together with only screws. Also remarkable was the large degree of prefabrication involved, especially clear with the sanitary units for the bathroom facilities. The construction method strongly resembled automobile construction as well—one of the models Prouvé had in mind for restructuring the construction industry with. The only problem with the otherwise remarkably stable building were the thermal movements of its metal façades. In winter the building contracted, in summer it expanded. As a result, the connections for the wall panels of 14.7 feet were subjected to an enormous amount of tension. A watertight surface could first be achieved by inserting strips of bitumen hidden under sheet metal at the connections.

The overall form of construction corresponded perfectly with the building's use. Seen today, it constitutes a manifesto of the modern age: avant-garde, technical, and rational. This might also explain why the general public took a strong interest in the building. The construction workers complained that having the site continually overrun with visitors kept them from finishing their work within the planned time limits.

Overall view with curtain wall façade

Right page below:
Detail of sheet-metal posts and double glazing

1935–1939 ▸ Maison du Peuple in Clichy
Eugène Beaudouin and Marcel Lods, architects

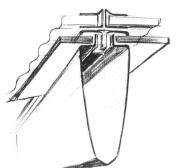

The Maison du Peuple (People's House), which represents a logical further development of the Aero Club, is clearly Prouvé's most important work. The two architects responsible for the building were Eugène Beaudouin and Marcel Lods.

In 1935, the local government of Clichy decided on the erection of a modern administration building. Alongside the administrative chambers, the building would also house assembly rooms and office spaces. The ground floor was to be left completely open to incorporate a roofed market. The upper floor, housing the assembly rooms, had to be flexible enough to convert into spaces for presentations, events with film screenings, and to service the opening to the ground floor.

Planned for the rear of the structure were the rooms for the labor union and offices of the city council. Because of the weekend market on the ground floor, there had to be a quick and efficient way of ventilating the building. For this purpose, Prouvé provided a glass roof that opened and closed when necessary. This simple construction was so well conceived that even today the roof still functions with its original parts.

Using demountable wall and floor elements, Prouvé succeeded at uniting in a single building what were at times vastly different spatial functions through intelligently conceived floor, roof, and wall elements able to be shifted. In Clichy, unlike the Aero Club near Versailles, a conventional-style supporting structure made of steel buttresses and supports was finally chosen. The structural engineers rejected Prouvé's first design for the supporting framework, intended to be carried out completely with welted sheet steel. Prouvé's reason for conceding was that the inspection authorities had no basis of calculation as yet for this new and sophisticated form of construction.

The entire building was conceived to leave the supporting structure and façade completely separated from one another. Apart from the building's prefabrication, simple assembly and primary building elements, the reason for doing this was the heat loss that could occur in lightweight buildings utilizing mixed construction methods. Even then Prouvé made sure that the respective detail fulfilled more than its primary function. In this case, the building's connection details not only held the façade in place, but also ensured that no heat loss occurred through an inflexible connection. The façade in Clichy was tried, tested and executed as one of the earliest of modern, curtain wall constructions, whose glass panels were secured by supporting members made of welted sheet metal. These details predicted Prouvé's later and far more complex constructions like the school façades in Villejuif, dating from the 1950s. That the façade panels of the Maison du Peuple were considerably smaller than those used for the Aero Club made them easier to transport and to install.

Sealing the joints was further improved by using a spring system with aluminum-laminated bitumen. This kept the construction completely weatherproof and able to withstand thermal tension, so that now Prouvé could also risk using a greater number of joints as construction and design elements.

Viewed from its construction alone, the building's planning and execution was very similar to the pavilion near Versailles. Seen in detail, however, elements such as the

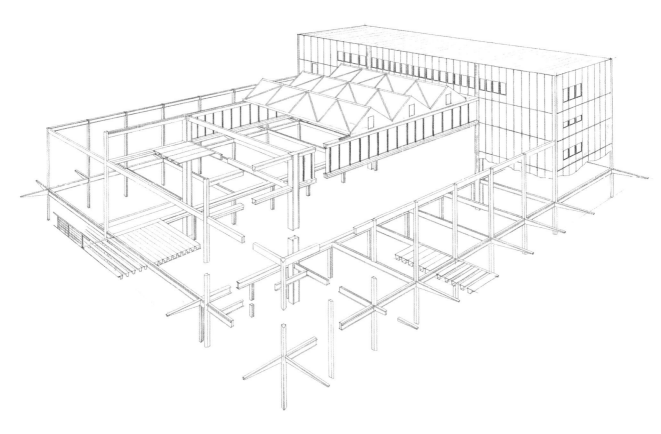

Design rendering; overall perspective

Right:
Design rendering; detail

prefabricated sanitary units, staircases, doors, and walls were far more developed. In Clichy, following the "private experiment" near Versailles, produced for the first time was a representative public building using a totally new, easily applied, and moisture-free construction method. The Maison du Peuple was the first project for which Prouvé gained enormous public recognition.

Recognized as the "triumph of sheet-steel construction," in 1983 the building was declared a historical landmark.

Interior view of upper floor with assembly room

1936 ▸ Classroom Table with Two Chairs
École Nationale Professionnelle de Metz

Classroom table for two students, variation from 1951

The combination table and chair for two students was developed from a series initially conceived for a 1935 commission received in connection with expanding and modernizing the École Nationale Professionnelle (E.N.P) in Metz.

The connecting of table and chair complies with Prouvés affinity for multifunctional building parts, also visible in other designs for his furniture and construction works. Again Prouvé formulated the solution so that a single structural part could assume several functions: here, for example, the number of legs the piece of combined classroom furniture stands on could be reduced from twelve to four. Every supporting element serves the table as well as chair leg. The construction consists of welted sheet steel. The tabletop is made of wood. The middle crossbar is a steel beam that diago-

Page from the Prouvé Studios' catalog, 1950

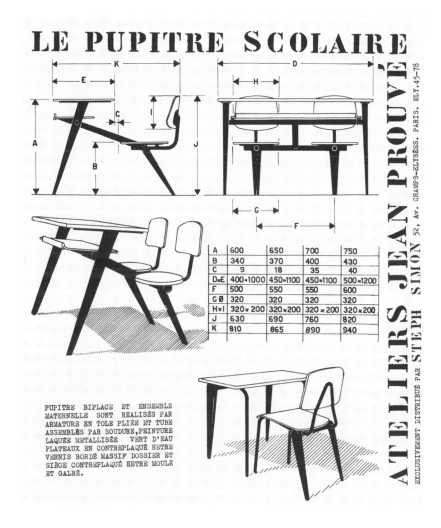

LE PUPITRE SCOLAIRE

ATELIERS JEAN PROUVÉ

EXCLUSIVEMENT DISTRIBUÉ PAR STEPH SIMON 52, AV. CHAMPS-ELYSÉES, PARIS. ELY.45—78

A	600	650	700	750
B	340	370	400	430
C	9	18	35	40
D×E	400×1000	450×1100	450×1100	500×1200
F	500	550	550	600
G Ø	320	320	320	320
H×I	320×200	320×200	320×200	320×200
J	630	690	760	820
K	810	865	890	940

PUPITRE BIPLACE ET ENSEMBLE
MATERNELLE SONT RÉALISÉS PAR
ARMATURE EN TOLE PLIÉE ET TUBE
ASSEMBLÉS PAR SOUDURE, PEINTURE
LAQUÉE METALLISÉE VERT D'EAU
PLATEAUX EN CONTREPLAQUÉ HETRE
VERNIS BORDÉ MASSIF DOSSIER ET
SIÈGE CONTREPLAQUÉ HETRE MOULÉ
ET GALBÉ.

Below:

Prototype of a one-seater classroom table, 1936

nally reinforces the table and supports the frame underneath the tabletop at the same time.

Like with many of Prouvé's creations, there exist numerous variations of this classroom table, which mainly differ with respect to the design of their seats (sometimes made of wood) and bedding planes. This particular model was so successful that it was produced in large numbers in different series.

The extremely dynamic appearance of Prouvé's combination table-and-chair design divulges his deep fascination with cars and airplanes.

1937 ▸ Garden Furniture for the U.A.M. Pavilion
Exposition internationale des Arts et Techniques, Paris
▸ with Jacques André

Left page:
View of the terrace of the U.A.M. pavilion with garden furniture, 1937

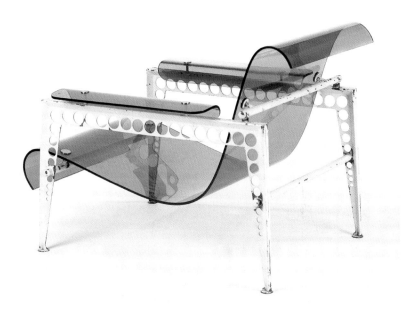

Garden chair, 1937

In 1937, for the exhibition "Exposition Internationale des Arts et Techniques de Paris," the U.A.M. (Union of Modern Architects) showcased its own exhibition pavilion. Cooperating with Jacques André, Prouvé designed its garden chairs and had them built in his workshops.

For the first time, Prouvé used perforated supporting elements made of steel for this furniture. The curved forms of the seats, until then atypical for his work, could have been based on ideas by André. The furniture was characterized by the use of a material known as "rhodoid"—a transparent synthetic on the basis of cellulose acetate, a compound originally known from photography production, and first used for architectural purposes at the 1937 World's Fair.

The knowledge gained from using this material was never directly explored afterwards: the synthetic material was either too expensive or too impractical. In the 1950s, however, Prouvé returned to the theme of perforations. It was taken up again, for example in the intricate wall panels of the Tropical Houses, where the perforations were used as ventilating openings. Although Prouvé categorically rejected an aesthetic based purely on style, the stylistic elements in his works nevertheless formed a clearly identifiable feature. This also made it easier to reckon with the perforations, finding their use at times in entrances and wall panels.

1939 ▸ Demountable Barrack Units

Prototype of the demountable barrack units for the Engineering Corps of the 5th Army, 1939
Testing the construction of the barrack in a Maxéville workshop

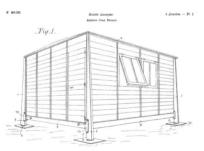

Bottom row:
Views of the barrack units; on the left a drawing used to file the patent application

In the autumn of 1939—with war already declared and periods of ceasefire yet to begin—Prouvé was called back from his vacation in Brittany by General Dumontier of the Engineering Corps of the 5th Army. Dumontier gave him the rush order to develop a type of barrack meant for twelve men and able to construct within a few hours. Prouvé worked day and night on the assignment, and within a week he presented a prototype of the demountable barracks to the general. For this project he made use of a construction principle that he had previously employed for the barracks of a young people's vacation resort in Onville: the barracks' load-bearing structure was a perimeter frame, lined with wooden panels. At the test run for assembling the barracks, conducted in Birkenwald in Alsace before the general staff, the time needed to build each structure amounted to no more than three hours. The French army ordered 275 of these barracks, but the production had to be stopped due to the German invasion.

1939–1947 ▸ Maisons à Portiques
S.C.A.L. in Issoire; Factory premises in Maxéville
▸ Charlotte Perriand and Pierre Jeanneret, architects

After the liberation of France, the "Jean Prouvé Studios" received a commission from the Minister for Reconstruction and Urban Planning, Raoul Dautry, to create 800 emergency accommodations for the war victims of Lorraine and the Vosges, and a contract was drawn up in June of 1945. But in the course of the assignment only about 400 of the intended demountable houses—the building type later called "maison à portiques"—were produced.

The demountable houses represented a further development of the demountable barrack units, and were also characterized by their quick and simply assembly. Buildings of this type were expected to satisfy certain requirements: they had to be trans-

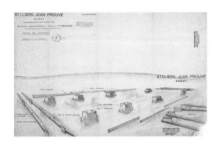 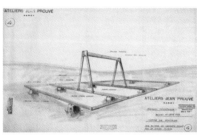 

Upper row:
Montage instructions for S.C.A.L. in Issoire, 1939–1940
The axially aligned grid frame construction ("portique") is clearly recognizable

Bottom row:
Demountable house with 19.7 x 19.7 feet floor plan

portable by truck (meaning no single building part would be longer than about 13 feet) and able to be assembled without large amounts of assistance (ideally requiring two trained workers); their joints and connections had to be tension-free in the event of thermal distortions; their façades made of exchangeable elements, and no individual building part was to be heavier than 100 kg. The power denudation had to be distributed over all the building parts.

The principle applied here had already been developed by Prouvé during the war—together with Charlotte Perriand and Pierre Jeanneret—for the aluminum manufacturer Sociéte Centrale des Alliages Léger (S.C.A.L.) in Issoire, near Clermont-Ferrand. Unlike with the demountable barrack units, the core of the static system was an axially-aligned frame construction made of sheet steel and featuring two supports in the form of an inverted V, whose structural framework resembles a child's swing. It practically

Pavilion 26.2 x 26.2 feet for the firm Permali in Maxéville, 1946
In this building phase, the house's simple and logical static system is detectable.

carried the weight of the roof on its own while also establishing the structure's diagonal and longitudinal reinforcement. As wooden panel constructions based on 3.3-feet-long modules of different widths, the walls were enhanced with windows. The modular construction method made it possible to exchange one element with another. As a result the buildings could be produced in different variations and sizes, depending on their designated function.

Also belonging to the "maisons à portiques" construction type were the buildings completed in 1944–1945 for the bakelized wood factory "Permali," as well as several buildings erected on the grounds of the "Jean Prouvé Studios" in Maxéville from 1946 to 1947, which include the main office as well the production and storage spaces. The office building was erected on a floor space of 26.2 x 26.2 feet. The floor plan was divided into a smaller section, housing two rooms and bathroom facilities, and a larger one, serving as a work space of 16.4 x 26.2 feet. In the larger section a 13.1-feet-long and room-height glazing allowed for a view of the premises. The entire building was a floor-mounted construction, whose unheated spaces underneath functioned as areas for storage and mechanical services. Office staff entered the building via an exterior staircase.

During the Maxéville period, Prouvé was at the zenith of his career both as a designer and manufacturer. In 1954, however, after the operation was taken over by Aluminium Français, Prouvé left his workshops and subsequently his office. He never set foot on the grounds again. The office building, classified as a historical landmark in 1987, was restored in 2002.

Prouvé's office on the workshop grounds in
Maxeville

Cover of the magazine *L'Architecture
d'aujourd'hui* No. 4, 1946

The prominent window enables a view over
the workshop grounds.

Prouvé with an Australian co-worker

1948–1951 ▸ Meridian Hall

Observatory Paris ▸ André Rémondet, architect

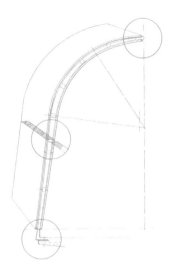

Above left:
System sketch of the connecting points for the montage work on the outer-skin elements

Above right:
Aerial view

Left page:
Pediment side of the main wing with circular openings for lighting and ventilation

The Meridian Hall (Salle Méridienne) of the Paris Observatory dates back to a design by the architect André Rémondet. Under Prouvé's constant supervision, the work on the hall was largely carried out by Jean Boutemain, a coworker of the Construction Department in Maxéville. The structure is made of three interconnected building parts arranged in a cross-like formation. Its main wing—53.8 feet long and completed as a rounded "only roof" construction in which the roof shrouds whole sides of a building down to its foundation—is based on a rectangular ground-floor plan that extends in an exact east-westerly direction. Flanking the main wing are the two square-shaped structural additions given flat roofs. The entire construction rests on a concrete foundation built on location.

The building's main wing is of the "voûte" (vaulted type). It is composed of a series of module segments, each consisting of two aluminum shells bolted together at their vertex. This accentuates the idea of a seamless transition from the wall to roof. The exterior sides of the roof are polished; the interior sides are smooth and varnished. Operating on tracks and a ball-bearing system, the individual roof segments can be rolled back far enough to reveal an unobstructed view of the sky.

The Meridian Hall demonstrates Prouvé's maxim to plan a project's overall production, and the application of its materials, as rationally as possible while using only a few and relatively simple elements. With only a single setting of the steel processing machinery, the elements produced for the hall served different functions simultaneously. The round openings in the walls, for example, were used for lighting as well as ventilating purposes. The observatory has a special status among Prouvé's works, because he completed no other "only roof" constructions during this period. Nevertheless, it represents an important step in the development of later works such as the shell ("coque") and shed-roof constructions.

1949 ▸ "Guéridon" Table

The "E.M." table developed from the "Guéridon" table system

In 1941, the first variation of the "Guéridon" table ("a small circular table") was already produced for the office of the chief engineer of the mining works in Nancy. Its serial production, however, first began in 1949, after World War II. Tables of this type are easily recognized by the triangular arrangement of their legs and star-shaped connecting elements made of steel. They generally have round tabletops. The unique appearance of the "Guéridon" tables dates back to Prouvé's design considerations from the 1930s.

Unlike the architectural avant-garde of that period, concerned with trying to create the illusion of a dissolving presence and transparency with highly polished sections of chrome steel (as with Marcel Breuer's cantilever furniture, or Le Corbusier's chaise longue), Prouvé's design approach compares more so with that of a design engineer. How the material bears its load as well as the distribution and disengagment of energies are made visible through an intensive reshaping of elements. Of central impor-

Café table variation of the "Guéridon" table

Below:
Detail of the steel-to-wood connection

tance here are the star-shaped joint bonds made of steel. They not only take on the moment of tension, but also transpose it visually. Prouvé's works are less characterized by their transparency, elegance, and lightness than they are by a sense of constructivism.

The "Guéridon" table was produced in numerous series, in a variety of materials, sizes, and forms. Special mention is given here to the "Guéridon cafeteria" model, employing a round tabletop usually made of metal and reaching the height of a conventional café table. Some of these models included a smaller tabletop-like board attached underneath the tabletop. Another variation was the "Guéridon Bas" ("Low Guéridon") model, conceived as a sofa table, with correspondingly compressed legs and a tabletop measuring 47.2 inches in diameter. Other "Guéridon" variations had rectangular tabletops and were named E.M. ("Entretoise Métallique") tables. The latest of the ongoing new editions of the "Guéridon" table appeared in 2001.

1949–1952 ▸ Standard Houses

Cité "Sans souci", Meudon
▸ Henri Prouvé and André Sive, architects

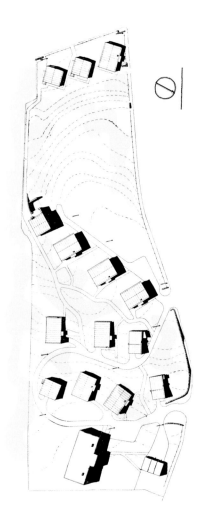

Site plan of the apartment colony in Meudon

Apartment house of the 26.2 x 26.2 feet type

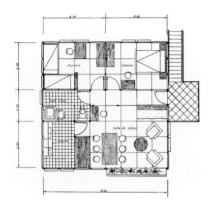

Floor plan of the 26.2 x 26.2 feet type

When French Minister Eugène Claudius-Petit, a friend and supporter of Prouvé's, visited the Maxéville workshops in 1949, this led to the Ministry of Reconstruction and Urban Planning (M.R.U.) granting Prouvé the assignment to develop a series of lightweight steel structures intended for mass production as houses. No single house was to cost more than the simplest of traditional-style suburban dwellings, and twenty-five structures of this type were immediately considered. They were meant to test whether the lightweight steel construction method could be used as a quick and economical remedy for the housing shortage in France.

The "maisons standard métropole" that Prouvé developed during the course of completing this commission belonged to the "maison à portique" building type. 25 buildings of this type were produced in the Maxéville workshops and awaited their construction. But the negotiations with the ministry dragged on, since the houses were clearly more expensive than structures built in the so-called conventional style. An agreement was finally reached to build ten "standard houses" (with four in the "coque" building style) in a park in Meudon, a suburb on the outskirts of Paris. The remaining fifteen "standard" buildings appeared at different locations throughout France and even in Algeria.

Variations on the standard house rest on a stone-built foundation designed by Prouvé's brother Henri

Assembly of a "standard" house type
Visible in the interior area are both frames in form
of an inverted U, with ridge beams. The ridge
beam is divided into segments to ensure that only
two workers are needed to assemble the house.

Interior view with U-shaped supports

Four of the "standard" houses completed in Meudon were erected on a 26.2 x 26.2 feet floor space, and the remaining six on a floor space of 26.2 x 39.3 feet. The principal structures of each house were the (one or two) welted sheet-steel structural frames in the form of an inverted U, on which a ridge beam rested. While bearing the central load, these frames also served as the primary structure during the building phase, and they made it possible for the remaining supporting elements of the house to be erected by a single person. Because of the modular system, based on 3.3-feet units, the exterior walls made of panels of aluminum sheet metal could accommodate doors, windows, and other permanent fixtures. The connections for the individual panels were contrived using sections of sheet metal. The roof was then placed atop to the supporting exterior walls.

At that time, this type of wall construction was considered unsually innovative. Viewed in detail, the ensured heat protection through the use of glass wool as an insulating material and the measures taken to avoid any thermal bridges were extremely effective. The reinforcing spring elements made of steel not only stabilized the individual wall panels, but also maintained the spacing between the inner and outer facings.

Interior view facing the dining area and
kitchen

Below:

**Detail drawing of the connection between the
frame, ridge beam, and roof**

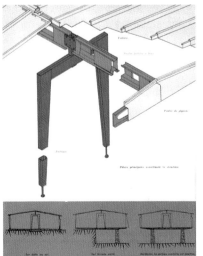

The fact that the buildings today are still in good condition says much for Prouvé's
detailed planning. Even if the housing estate's success remains open to dispute, it can
nevertheless be said that the residents were satisfied with these houses and—with
some having lived here from the very beginning—many have remained to the present
day. The only problem they have concerns finding original replacement parts for the
buildings, which compares with the equally difficult task of finding parts for an old-
timer.

Testing the construction of a building section
on the Maxéville workshop grounds, 1949

Below:
Sectional drawing

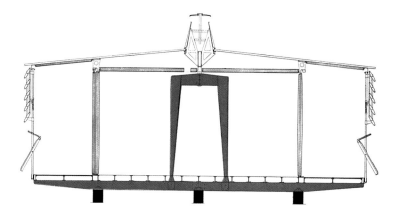

1949 ▸ Houses for the Tropics
Niamey, Niger and Brazzaville, Congo ▸ Henri Prouvé, architect

Three upper photos:
**Unloading building parts from the plane in Niamey, Niger, 1949;
Construction of a house in Niamey, 1949;
Assembled houses in Brazzaville, 1951**

In 1949, together with his brother Henri, Prouvé produced the first "maison tropicale" for the chancellor of the University of Niamey in Niger. This would be the prototype for an entire series of well thought-out and easy to assemble houses. With these structures, Prouvé intended to prove a specific point: compared to the local constructions, his prefabricated buildings were better suited to the climate, and they could also be built in less time. However, Prouvé failed to demonstrate this point: the "maisons tropicales" proved too expensive, and also their production lasted too long. As a result, only two more buildings of this type were built, both in Brazzaville, in the Congo: one accommodated the regional Information Office of the aluminum manufacturer Studal, and the other offices of the Ministry of Education.

As a further development of the "maisons à portiques" structures of the previous years, the "maisons tropicales" undoubtedly create the height of the series of houses of the "standard" type. With their 32.8 x 45.9 feet floor space, these buildings are based on a grid of 3.3-feet-long units as well. The entire construction is conceived to allow its individual parts to be delivered by plane—another decisive argument being here their quick delivery.

Prouvé devised a special system for making these load-bearing framed structures suitable for tropical and subtropical climates: the house is provided with a 19.7-feet-wide and 39.4-feet-long cella-like interior space. This space is surrounded by a peripheral space (3.3 feet wide at its front faces, with sides of 6.6 feet) contained by a second outer enclosure for the building. The second enclosure allows the house to stand at all times in its own self-made shade. To facilitate an additional cooling down of the house's "inner cella," the second enclosure also features a chimney—like opening in the roof's inner ceiling, which guarantees permanent air circulation. The cut of the house makes especially visible the relationship between its static construction and climate control system. The principal load-bearers for the inner cella-like space are two central supports made of steel, constructed in the form of an inverted U, and the incurring load is directly carried by the exterior walls. Each of these walls can be generously opened, using the respective five sliding doors on their longer sides and the large two-winged doors in their front faces. When the walls are closed, the interior space receives light and air through round openings in the sliding doors.

Both the originality and the well thought-out conception of the "maisons tropicales" are what make them so fascinating even today. In 2001, in the throes of the civil war disputes, former American Minister of Finance Robert Rubin instigated a spectacular rescue operation for one of the buildings, whose elements were partly riddled with bullets: he had it transported from Brazzaville to Paris, where it could be erected again with the help of experts.

1950 ▸ School in Vantoux

Henri Prouvé, architect

Above:
View of the instructors' building

Right:
Classes in session in the school building

When the economic situation in France in 1949 demanded immediate and inexpensive building solutions, the French Ministry of Education announced a competition for the designing of an industrialized type of school building. Working together with his brother Henri, Prouvé won the competition. Yet their submitted design was implemented only twice: once for a school in Bouqueval, and a second time in Vantoux, near Metz. These types of school buildings use the same static system found in "standard house" and "maison tropicale" structures, and they represent another variation of the "maison à portique".

The sloped building site for the school in Vantoux had to be fully terraced in advance. The relatively small school was divided into a building for the instructors and another for students. All the school's building components were prefabricated at

Left page:
View of the student's building

Prouvé's workshops and assembled "dry" on location. The instructors' building was situated somewhat higher than the wing for the classrooms. The students' building was completely sealed at the rear and given a front face with windows facing south. The exterior walls were yellow, and those of the interior spaces a brighter shade of red, creating a friendly atmosphere. This also established a clear contrast between the simplicity of the construction and its industrial appearance.

Even though society at that time was highly skeptical of the industrialized building method, today the building still ranks as a historical landmark.

1950–1951 ▸ Grand Palais of the Lille Fairgrounds

**Paul Herbé and Maurice Louis Gauthier, architects;
Désiré Douniaux, engineer**

**Picture postcard of the Lille Fairgrounds
building, 1950s**

Built in 1934 by the architects Paul Herbé and Maurice Louis Gauthier, this building served as the exhibition hall for the City of Lille in the North of France. Severely damaged during World War II, the construction received the needed repairs and was rebuilt in 1951 on the occasion of the International Textile Exhibition. The engineer Désiré Douniaux, who oversaw the façade's construction, devised for it a 8.2-feet-deep supporting structure suitable for the hanging of advertisements. In the middle of 1950, Prouvé was commissioned to supervise the details and execution of the construction work.

Divided into vertically arranged hole-embedded supports and horizontal joint bonds, the entire construction rested on tapering supports made of steel that marked the entranceways. The façade was composed of 990 massive, glazed panels, all of which had to be precisely calculated and inserted. Prouvé's workshops were also given the job of completing the doors, grasping elements, and ticket booth for the Grand Palais.

Considered from the radical disclosure of its structural concept, the Grand Palais de la Foire can be seen as the forerunner of many modern buildings, for example of the

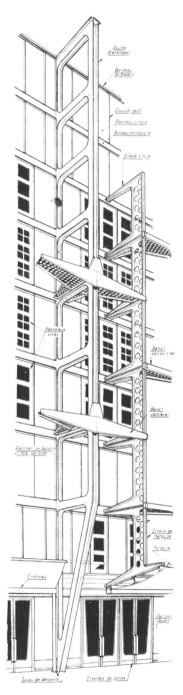

Centre Pompidou in Paris (Renzo Piano, Richard Rogers, Gianfranco Franchini) and Lloyd's Bank in London (Richard Rogers). It served as a model for a great many high-tech buildings whose supporting structures were aesthetically engaged as expressive elements in their constructions. In 1987, this fascinating building was torn down during the course of the preparations for the Euralillie Project. In his catalogue raisonné on Prouvé's works, the author Peter Sulzer comments on the building's demise by writing: "[It] was the vanishing of an architectural masterpiece!"

1950–1952 ▸ Shed Roofs for the Mame Printing Works
Tours ▸ Drieu-La-Rochelle and Bernard Zehrfuss, architect

Left page:
Shed roofs of the Mame printing works

Right:
Interior view of the printing works

Below:
The system was conceived to be built by only two works using a lifting device.

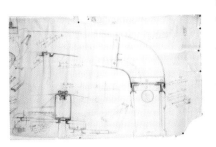

Sketch of a wall-to-roof connection point
The rounded corners avoided the use of any exceptional connection points.

Following the work carried out on the Meridian Hall of the Paris Observatory, Prouvé was soon preoccupied with the question of how to create a joint-free connection between a roof and wall—traditionally a complicated transition. With this objective in mind, he developed the bent, shell-like form known as a "coque," first put to use in shed-roof constructions. These completely prefabricated elements, often as long as 16.4 feet, together with their insulation, protective sheeting, and their outer and inner skin, were light enough to be assembled by only two workers. In 1950 Prouvé was granted a patent on "prefabricated roof elements".

In the same year, the Tour-based Mame Printing Works hired the Maxéville workshops to renovate their facilities. Between 1950 and 1952 a total of 672 shell-element components were built into its roofs.

In 1952–1953 Prouvé received yet another commission from the Mame Printing Works. On the flat roof of the printing works' administrative building, he developed a series of pavilion-like structures whose established connection between a roof and wall was also based on the "coque" system. These satisfied all the needs of an administrative floor, and housed the office of the owner, an assembly room, and a sun lounge, among other spaces.

1950–1952 ▸ Maisons coques

Salon des Arts Ménagers, Paris; Cité "Sans souci", Meudon

Interior view of a residential pavilion based on the "coque" system and shown at the Exposition de l'Habitation in the Salon des Arts Ménagers, in Paris, 1951

During the assembly work for the Mame Printing Works, Prouvé made an observation that he later described as follows: "One beautiful day, around lunchtime, I saw thirty workers taking a break. They were sitting and eating among the stored shed-roof elements—and they all told me the same thing: 'We don't know why, but we feel at ease here.'" This was the birth of the shell houses or "maisons coques," whose prototype Prouvé presented in Paris at the 1951 exhibition Arts Ménagers. Basically, this construction principle entailed no more than creating a series of "shells" made of bent shed-roof elements, which rest on façades or interior walls. Not much later, numerous variations on such "shell houses" were completed.

This was the same year that Prouvé tried selling to the innovative automobile manufacturer Citroën a series of apartment houses developed on the basis of the "coque" system, intended as living spaces for the company's employees. He speculated most with Citroën's marked interest in the "modern," as demonstrated in the prefabricated construction method used for manufacturing its "2CV" model (nicknamed "The Duck"), the new car presented at the 1949 Automobile Salon in Paris. The

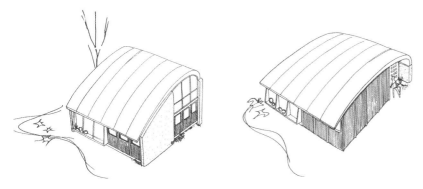

Drawing of the apartment houses designed for car manufacturer Citroën

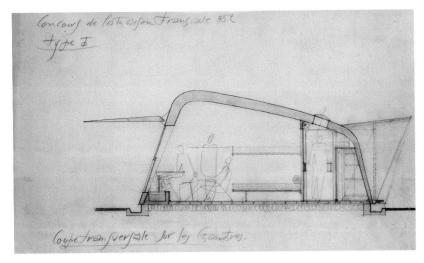

Above left:
Exterior view of a residential pavilion based on the "coque" system, shown at the Exposition de l'Habitation in the Salon des Arts Ménagers, in Paris, 1951

Above right:
Model of the two-storey house for Citroën

Below left:
Design sketch of the "coque" house type, circa 1950

buildings Prouvé proposed were meant to be economical and prefabricated and able to be assembled over the weekend by the users themselves.

These structures evinced a fascinating further development of the "coque" principle, applied at first only on shed roofs. Here, too, the construction principle was based on the idea of a roof and wall forming a single building part. This was the type of shell house that Prouvé presented to Citroën's management in two variations: the first, an enclosed pavilion, could be expanded in succession using additional "coque" modules; the second, a two-storey single home, was conceived for as many as four people. But Prouvé's initial hopes were quickly undone: the company's management firmly told him that the houses were "too modern".

In spite of the setback, houses of this type were further developed in Maxéville just the same. Around a year later, an entire series of shell-house apartments had been produced. In 1952, four shell houses were built in a small experimental colony in

A house in Meudon based on the "coque"
system

Below:
Interior view

Meudon. These were executed in two different versions. The first version involved houses using a single shell, resting on one side on a façade, enclosed between two brick-built flank walls; the second combined a pair of directionally opposed shells, supported by the carrying brick-built elements. Yet the houses erected in Meudon depicted a watered down version of the "coque" principle, precisely because of the excessive amount of masonry work in the constructions.

1951–1952 ▸ Lecture Hall Chair
University of Aix-Marseilles, Aix-en-Provence

In 1952, Prouvé designed and produced a chair for the lecture hall of the University of Aix-Marseilles. Its design shows that Prouvé had developed a personal and unconventional formal language with regard to confronting metal. It also points out how creative a design can be in and of itself, even when using a limited number of materials. Forming a unity with the chair's legs, the back of the chair is made of welted sheet steel. Like with classic American classroom chairs, this chair, too, features a retractable book rest made of wood that can be folded away to the side. The reinforcing steel crossbar under the seat bears a strong structural resemblance to the "Compas" table. In all his works, Prouvé chose to work with standardized building components, which saved on production costs and additional customizing.

Lecture Hall of the University of Aix-Marseille
with seating

Strikingly different about this chair is its unconventionally formed back rest—something difficult to explain when studying the design sketches. In fact, no clear explanation for Prouvé's chair design seems to exist. His daughter, Catherine Prouvé, voiced the assumption that the chair's soft and flexible appearing building parts, together with its dynamic backward thrust when viewed in profile, might have been the result of

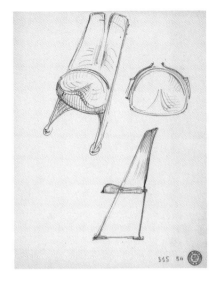

Design sketches for the Lecture Room Chair

Right:
The Lecture Room Chair

her father's habit of "titling himself" on the back legs of a chair when seated. This habit might even explain how the Standard Chair got its well-developed back legs. Another explanation for the lecture hall chair's unusual form could be that Prouvé wanted to free the spine from the innate conditions of the back as a way to avoid fatigue while listening.

1953 ▸ "Compas" Table

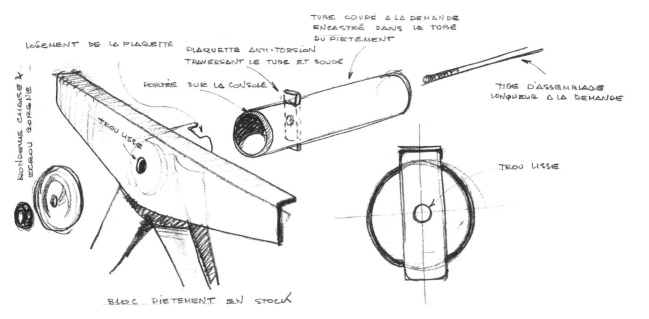

LOGEMENT DE LA PLAQUETTE

RONDELLE CHASSÉ & ÉCROU BORGNE

TROU LISSE

PORTÉE SUR LA CONSOLE

PLAQUETTE ANTI-TORSION TRAVERSANT LE TUBE ET SOUDÉ

TUBE COUPÉ À LA DEMANDE ENCASTRÉ DANS LE TUBE DU PIETEMENT

TIGE D'ASSEMBLAGE LONGUEUR À LA DEMANDE

TROU LISSE

BLOC PIETEMENT EN STOCK

Design drawing
Prouvé tended to emphasize the montage procedure in his designs.

Left page above:
"Compas" table

Left page below:
"Compas" table variation

Developed in 1953, the "Compas" table was produced in several variations. Although one of Prouvé's sketches points to the table being designed as part of a system that could be disassembled, this idea was never further pursued.

The table's construction is based on an axis created by round tubing that functions both as a connecting element for the table legs and as a support for the tabletop. While the round tubing absorbs the bulk of the resulting torque moments, the table legs bear only the load of the tabletop. The relatively large dimensions chosen for the tubing gives the table its distinctive appearance. Its tapering legs and support elements form the opposite poles to the heaviness of the devised connection, so that at the table's massive connecting point all the incurring energies become technically resolved as well as visualized.

The original model was asymmetrical, in the sense that the tabletop protruded more at one side than at the other. One variation was the café table, in which a supporting crossbeam is mounted underneath the tabletop at its center, and another the classroom table, featuring larger tables for teachers and smaller ones for students. In addition, there were the "Compas" models with rectangular and round tabletops made of wood, steel, or Plexiglas. The table's frame was even used as the basis for completing a bench design.

1953–1954 ▶ Prouvé Residence
Nancy

Left page:
Jean Prouvé in the living room of his private residence
He sits in an armchair conceived for the Cité Universitaire in Nancy. In the foreground is a table of the "Guéridon" type.

Right:
View along the bedroom wing facing the living room

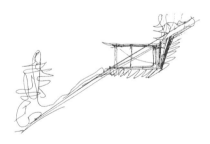

Sketch of the sloped site for the house

The house that Jean Prouvé built for his family is an exception among his other works. It was produced as a never-varied unique structure without duplicates. Built on the slope of a hill, it has a view of the City of Nancy. The site at Prouvé's disposal was "simple and overgrown—and rather deserted, because no one wanted to live on such sloped property." It posed a great challenge for the building of a house, not to mention the slanted earth's high content of sand and loose pebbles.

Because of his limited financial means, Prouvé built the house using the remaining parts from his never completed projects. These parts—he liked calling them "leftovers"—were largely the elements for emergency accommodations produced around that time in the Maxéville workshops. In addition, building parts from other series were incorporated and reworked for this purpose. But a few elements, such as the roof of the house, were custom-made for the project. The construction workers responsible for erecting the house were supported over the weekend by Prouvé's family and friends. For this reason, too, Prouvé referred to the undertaking as being "a little botched up".

In reality, the building was originally intended as a "maison coque" structure. But after changing his focus at that time, Prouvé felt more inclined to lend the construction a greater lightness. As a result, the roof came to be made of panels, which rest on thin supports made of metal. The house is a one-storey construction. Within its extending

pavilion, which reaches a length of 88.5 feet, the rooms are lined up one after the other. The back wall forms the principal load-bearing element for the structure's face supports by means of raised, steel rectangles (23.6 inches in width). Running the back wall's full length is a built-in wardrobe and shelving unit. An embedded floor heating is installed in floor slabs, composed of thin metal supports that rest on underbases as well as concrete. The façade elements surfaced with wood originate, in part, from Prouvé's "standard house" series, and the wall elements, with their perforation-like window and ventilation openings, from his "maison tropicale" series. Built facing south, the façade of the living room is completely glass-enclosed. Prouvé had already given much thought to the solar radiation and the resulting energy to be extracted from it.

The massive side walls built of stone give the house the needed stability for enduring strong winds, and the inner walls are lined with wood. A special feature are the door openings with rounded corners, similar to those in a ship, indicating raised thresholds. Instead of resulting from any daring aesthetic impulses, this solution is specifically geared to the possible settings of the processing machinery: working through the rounded corners and raised thresholds, the machinery had only to be engaged once, and cutting out the door opening could be completed with a single cut. This helped to avoid having to constantly reset the machinery, which meant saving on manual labor, production costs, and time. While designing the house, the sizes of the actual rooms took on a special significance. Here Prouvé divulges the basic principle that the children's rooms should take up only a minimum of space. For one of his children, he calculated that an area measuring 6.6 x 9.8 feet sufficed for a single room:

Floor plan

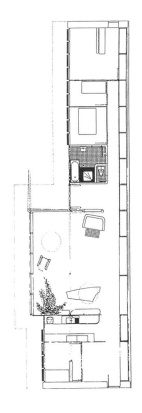

this allowed for a standardized bed, writing table, and bookshelf. A double room had to make due with an area measuring 9.8 x 9.8 feet. The parents' bedroom was somewhat larger. Limiting the private spaces in the house allowed for a larger living-room area, which reflected Prouvé's great passion for entertaining the many guests who often stayed over.

1953–1954 ▸ Façade of the Apartment Building on Mozart Square

Paris ▸ Lionel Mirabeau, architect

The original state of the façade with vertical sheet-metal reinforcements

System sketch of the connection between posts and glazing

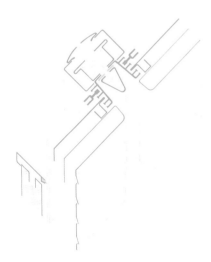

In 1953–1954, the apartment building on Mozart Square in Paris was erected by the architect Lionel Mirabeau as a steel-and-concrete and masonry work construction. Prouvé oversaw the designing and execution of its façades. Unique about the façades are their moveable window elements. These adapt themselves to the respective weather conditions and assume a variety of positions: on overcast days, they allow the windows sections to be fully opened; on sunny days, their awning-like constructions create shade, and at night they completely seal off the window openings. The guillotine windows move parallel to every assumed position of the shading elements. Located behind the windows, a parapet panel handles the heat insulation in this area. The parapet and façade elements are hung before the outer edge of the concrete ceiling, with vertically-arranged welted seams providing their reinforcement. Because this detail was either overlooked or misunderstood during the renovating of the façades, a "twisting" of the elements occurred, which also led to an inconsistent appearance.

Regarding the apartment building on Mozart Square, the artist Hervé Martin said that the repetition of the industrial generated by the façades "creates an entirely new aesthetic based on functional necessities." Indeed the diversity of the elements and their variations reveal a technical poetry all their own.

Left page:
Condition after the rehabilitation, photograph taken in 2005

1954 ▸ Pavilion for the centennial of Aluminum
Paris ▸ Henri Hugonnet and Armand Copienne, engineers

Overall view of the building showing its complete length of 492.1 feet

After Prouvé took leave of his Maxéville workshops Aluminum Français commissioned him to plan and execute a pavilion for "The Hundred Years of Aluminum Celebration" in Paris. This structure would serve as the exhibition hall for presenting the history of aluminum while also embodying the latest technological advancements in the field. Since no office space could be made available to Prouvé, all the planning took place in the conference room of the Aluminum Français. Thinking back, Prouvé claimed that this was the bitterest period of his professional life. Just the same, and perhaps for that very reason, the pavilion marks a distinct height in Prouvé's works.

The fact that the pavilion for the Hundred Years of Aluminum Celebration was executed without the collaboration of an architect makes it one of the few purely Prouvé-conceived buildings. In Paris, on the left bank of the Seine, a site only 82 feet wide was at Prouvé's disposal for building the pavilion. With the assistance of the engineers Henri Hugonnet and Armand Copienne, the resulting structure was 492 feet long and 49.2 feet wide. Positioned within a grid of 4.4 feet, the supporting buttresses were arranged in threes, in 13.1-feet-long sections. Stretched over the building's width of 49.2 feet, the roof supports served a second, typical-for-Prouvé function: designed

System sketch of the support structure

Right:
Pediment side

Design drawing

View of the reconstructed building near Paris,
2005

Right:
Detail view of the connection between the
massive roof girders and slender supports

Exterior view, 2005

The façade was glazed down to its base. The rear of the building developed to a projecting roof.

in the form of roof gutters, they permitted rainwater to be drained off at the same time. As further proof of Prouvé's great craftsmanship, the joining elements between the horizontal supports and the buttresses behind them were brilliantly conceived inventions. These uniquely designed connecting points transferred the energies of the heavy roof supports to slender buttresses, whose base points also created a contrast with the spaciousness of the pavilion's exhibition hall. Developed as finely structured joints, they lent the space a vivid sense of weightlessness. This refinement in the pavilion's construction endowed its hall with an almost breathtaking expression of lightness.

After it was disassembled in 1956, the hall experienced various changes of fate. In 1987, in a greatly altered state, it reappeared in Lille, but was removed again during the preparations for Rem Koolhaas' Euralille Project in the early 1990s, and its individual parts were put in storage. Even though the building was later classified an historic monument in 1993, it was first reassembled again in 2000, courtesy of the firm of SIPAC in Villepinte, with its length reduced to 249.3 feet.

1954 ▶ "Antony" Chair
Cité universitaire d'Antony

Left page:
Rearview of the chair

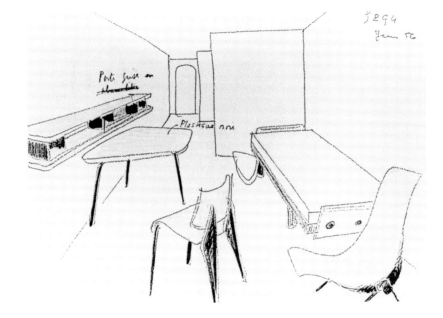

Design sketches of the "Antony" chair with other furniture designs by Prouvé

Since no sketches for it exist today, the "Antony" chair is hard to place chronologically. A few sources set the date of its creation at around 1950, when Prouvé and Charlotte Perriand participated in a competition on the occasion of developing new furniture for a part of the University of Strasbourg. The only definite dates originate from the Prouvé Archive, and these place the chair's production in the year 1954. According to the archive's information, Prouvé designed the chair on the occasion of a competition for creating new seating for the Cité Universitaire in Antony, a suburb of Paris.

The chair displays a fascinating combination of Prouvé's static-related and constructional ideas as used, for example, in the "Compas" table; in different chair designs, and instances where a constructional refinement served to disengage enormous amounts of energy, a fine example of this being how the roof support for "The Hundred Years of Aluminum Celebration" pavilion in Paris was finally expressed. The basis unit of the chair consists of a dynamically curved, supporting construction that bears the load similar to the way that this occurs in the "Compas" table: by means of steel tubing, the torque moments are absorbed by the chair legs. The curved, wooden seat of the chair attaches to the supports at four, hard to recognize points and gives the impression, as though a sail, that it floats over the supporting elements.

1955–1956 ▸ House for Abbé Pierre
Paris

After finding a woman frozen to death in the streets of Paris in the winter of 1954, clergyman Abbé Pierre, known for his charity work, and the organization that he founded, "Les Compagnons d'Emmaüs," launched an initiative to provide housing for the poorest of citizens. They received financial support from the detergent manufacturer Persil. Using as its motto "Les jours meilleurs" (The Better Days), shortened to "J.M.," the initiative's goal was to build 200 family houses meant to be financed through donations and Persil coupons. Every coupon found on the back of a box of Persil detergent and mailed back to the Emmaüs partners contributed to erecting the buildings. On this occasion, Abbé Pierre approached Prouvé with the plea to develop a system that would enable a large number of economical family houses to be built as quickly as possible.

Prouvé designed a building that was a variation on the type of family house developed together with his coworker Maurice Silvy in Maxéville—an "Alba" (aluminum-béton armé). Characteristic of the construction principle for this type of house is having a sanitary core rest on a sunken foundation of cast-in-place concrete. In Alba houses, this was made of reinforced concrete; in the house for Abbé Pierre, however, it was completely prefabricated and made of metal. Called a "monobloc," this core section not only housed a kitchenette, bath, and toilet; it also functioned as a support measure. In 1935 Prouvé had already used the preformed units of such sanitary blocks for the bathroom facilities of the Aero Club near Versailles. The house that he designed for Abbé Pierre had a floor space of only 559.8 square feet. It offered two bedrooms, a multifunctional living room immediately entered through the front door, and designated areas for living, eating, and cooking.

On February 21, 1956, at the Quay of Alexandre III on the Seine, assembling the prototype of the house proved to be a spectacular event. It lasted longer than the

Installing the "monobloc"
Visible in the photograph are the kitchen's built-in cabinets together with sink and cooking utensils.

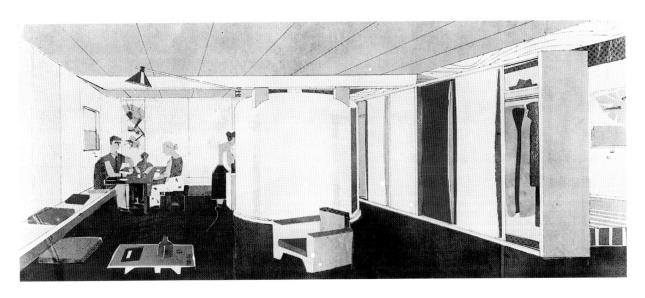

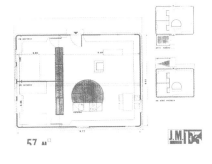

Floor plan

Left page above:
The completed building on Quai Alexandre III in Paris

scheduled seven hours, because so many people among the onlookers insisted on lending a hand to the two workers responsible for the construction. In any case, the press reported that on the following day Persil had received one million coupons.

This project unites essential aspects of Prouvé's main concerns: he hoped to create buildings that would be used by a maximum of one generation, and he envisioned the children of the first house owners reusing parts of the old constructions (their parents' houses) to build their own accommodations—citing here, for example, the "mono-bloc" cells. Prouvé incorporated ecological aspects in his design as well. Building houses that could be disassembled allowed the site to be sealed closed with buildings for an entire generation; but after these buildings were torn down, the site could be cleared, and the ground unsealed again.

The House for Abbé Pierre represents a successful example of space-saving and economical building practices. At that time, however, such a house seemed too radical, and it failed to meet with the approval of the housing authorities, also because of the sanitary core positioned in the middle of the living room. For that reason, its serial production never came about.

1956 ▸ Cachat Pump-Room in Evian
Évian-les-Bains ▸ Maurice Novarina, architect; Serge Kétoff, engineer

Overall view

During the brief period of working freelance that followed his leaving the workshops in Maxéville, Jean Prouvé ran a Paris-based office in the Rue de Louvois. This was when he received the assignment to construct and execute a design by the architect Maurice Novarina for a pump-room in the City of Évian on Lake Geneva. For this project, Prouvé gained the support of his coworker Jean Boutemain and engineer Serge Kétoff. The structure was built on a sloped site. Facing south, the completely glassed-in principal façade was enhanced by glass sliding doors. Built in front of this was a terrace of gener-ous dimensions. The steel construction rested on a massive concrete foundation sur-faced with natural stone in which adjoining spaces such as the bathroom facilities and kitchen were installed.

    This project focused on Évian's mineral water source is a special example of the "béquilles" or "crutch support" system that Prouvé developed. The building is com-posed of a series of asymmetrical, Y-shaped principal load-bearing elements (hence the expression "crutches" or "béquilles"), whose jointed base points, appearing in 19.7-feet increments along its longer sides, connect in pairs by way of a beam. Each "Y"

The crutch-like supports accentuate the span of the roof.

is held in place by thin tension supports. The remaining building elements are attached to this remarkably stabile frame construction, which enables a lateral span of 49.2 feet. This also explains why the tension supports could be so thin. The principal load-bearing elements appear massive and extensive at first glance, but they take on a lightness by virtue of a tapering termination point. Rising from a height of 13.8 to 17 feet, the dynamic of the hall's portable roof is created by their asymmetrically arranged supports. The astounding delicacy of the construction, and the playful handling of gravity in particular, make it seem as though the building ignores the laws of equilibrium.

1957 ▸ Temporary School Building in Villejuif
Serge Kétoff, engineer

Overall view

Among Prouvé's lesser-known works are the interim structures that he realized for a school in Villejuif, a suburb of Paris. This body of work involves altogether three buildings, each with a roofed-over schoolyard, two of which accommodate seven rooms, and the last only four. Like for the refreshment hall in Évian, Prouvé used the "béquille" construction principle for these school buildings, all of which can be disassembled. In this case, the portable roof rested on T-shaped "crutch" supports, secured by tension joints that served as reinforcement elements for the glass façade at the same time. Because the building was based on a 5.7-feet-wide module. The rise of the portable roof began at 8.2 feet on the side of the school where the corridor was located and ended at 10.8 feet meters on the unsupported side with the classrooms.

Aware of the building's thermal requirements, Prouvé provided for a roof overhang of more than three feet. This guaranteed the necessary shade for the classrooms. All the tension joints, which simultaneously functioned as ventilating elements for the classrooms, had V-shaped sections that faced inward. The lateral walls of the supports had perforations that opened and closed and regulated the air circulation in the rooms.

Interior view with crutch-like supports

Below:
Sketch for a school

After completing the planned school in a solid construction method, the interim structure was disassembled again. In individual segments, its fate was distributed throughout France.

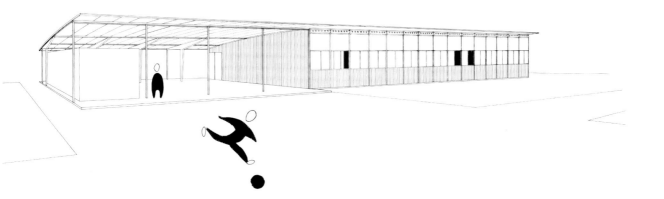

1961–1962 ▸ Seynave Vacation House

Beauvallon ▸ Neil Hutchinson, architect

Exterior view

Left page:
View from the children's room to the terrace on the right hand side and the living zone on the left

The vacation house is located in the South of France on the Côte d'Azur, near the Bay of St. Tropez. Until the late nineteenth century, this belt of land was a much-loved winter residence for the aristocracy and members of the upper middle class alike. Between the 1920s and 1960s, having so many affluent citizens build vacation domiciles here also gave a boost to tourism in the region. Prouvé received the commission to design the vacation house from a Lorraine-based paper manufacturer for whom he had already produced furnishings for his factory spaces. Prouvé planned and completed the house together with the young architect Neil Hutchinson.

Like the house designed for Abbé Pierre, this house, too, is a variation of the house type called "Alba". The building's supporting structure, consisting of concrete elements in its interior area, also forms parts of the kitchen, bathroom facilities, and wardrobe elements. The horizontal supports resting on these core elements are carried by detached and filigree steel supports. The remaining walls of the house consist of exposed wood panels; these playfully interact with contrasting, raw concrete components painted white and steel supports painted red. The outer skin is made of exposed

wood elements, rhythmically interchanged with expansive sliding doors made of glass and horizontally-arranged glass elements that serve ventilation purposes. The rounded corners increase the sensation of this being an open ground-floor plan, and they stand in contrast to the angular roof of the house. The floor plan was conceived as an unrestricted open area in which the zones of utilization are defined by an inward and outward-changing spatial emphasis.

Through the originality of its ground-floor plan and a construction method both elegant and intelligent, the simplicity as well as ingenuity of the structure uniquely interprets the theme of a modern vacation domicile. In 1990 private funding made it possible for the building to be expertly reconstructed in its original form. Recognized as an historic landmark since 1993, it now stands protected by preservation laws.

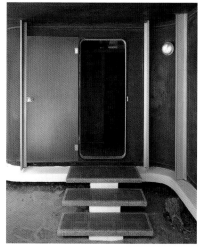

View of the unitized kitchen and buttery hatch

Right:
Floor plan

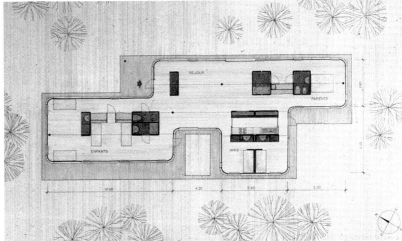

Left below:
Entrance

1962 ▶ Gauthier House
Saint-Dié ▶ Baumann and Remondino, architects

Exterior view towards entrance area

In 1962 Prouvé received the assignment to build a family house in Saint Dié from his daughter, Françoise, who was married to the doctor Pierre Gauthier and had four small children at that time. The designs for the Gauthier residence were developed together with the architects Bauman and Remondino.

The building is constructed according to the "Alba" principle, making it similar to both the house for Abbé Pierre and Seynave Vacation House. Located in the center of its concrete foundation is a massive core containing the kitchen and bathroom. Like in other projects, the roof's principal load-bearing supports rest on this core. Situated on an overhang, the house has a view of the city. Its basic structure is divided into a zone for living and another for sleeping, arranged to the left and right of the massive "wet room" core. In the living area, a large glazing offers an unobstructed view along the slope of a hill. The outer walls consist of a double-shell construction: on their inner as well as outer sides, the linings are formed by grooved aluminum plates, between which extruded polystyrene provides heat insulation. The ceilings are surfaced with wood. The floors are lined with ceramic tiles, and a roof overhang offers protection from the sun.

Interior view of living area

Right below:
Floor plan
The massive concrete core (accentuated gray tones) divides the structure into conventional sleeping and living areas.

Below :
Entrance door

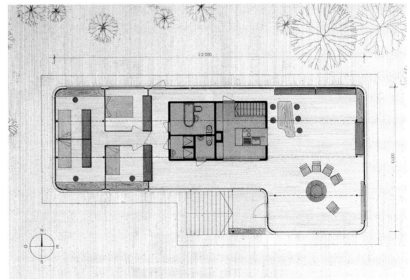

1967 ▸ Youth Center in Ermont

The complete facility

In 1967 the Ministry of Youth and Sports announced a competition for building 1,000 youth clubs to be erected throughout France. According to one of the competition's stipulations, it had to be possible for the clubs' future users to erect the structures themselves. Prouvé's design, developed in collaboration with C.I.M.T., was awarded first prize. Yet it was implemented only once, in Ermont (Val-d'Oise). After that, the Youth Center Program was cancelled.

The building of the type „voûte" is composed of two structural parts connected by a bridge in their upper floors. Prouvé used a vault in full centre, divided into two semi-circles with a 16.4-feet radius for each part, fusing wall and roof elements into a single building part to avoid any problematic connections. The individual roof and wall elements are 3.3 feet wide and able to be assembled in only 45 minutes by laymen. In addition, the completely assembled individual segments are placed on supporting tracks that rested on support elements made of concrete. The outer skin is made of aluminum and its inner surface of plywood. The innovation involved here was the foaming over of the sandwich element with polyurethane in order to guarantee more effective

Interior views

heat insulation. The elements are held together by simple screwed joints, and a squeezed weatherproofing of neoprene prevents the intrusion of moisture.

The ends of both structures terminate at walls made of acrylic glass, called "Altuglass". Their façades are compositionally divided by visually pronounced vertical reinforcing window supports utilizing only a single and relatively thin horizontal joint bond. For financial reasons the only elements that could be opened are the doors of the entrances on both floors. Since the highest point in the buildings allowed for an additional space reaching a height of 16.4 feet, it was possible to include a detached mezzanine. Free-standing inner walls of plywood serve as spatial dividers. For reasons of rationalizing the work process, like with Prouvé's private residence, the wooden "ship-doors" have raised thresholds.

This building not only documents Prouvé's wealth of ideas, but also points to his relentless search for new solutions.

1967–1969 ▸ Tour Nobel
Puteaux-La Défense
▸ Jean de Mailly and Jacques Depussé, architects

Rounded corner connection of the façade

Lying in the extension of the Parisian axe historique—the axis that connects the Louvre with the Arc de Triomphe via the Champs-Élysées, and already passes beyond the compacted inner-city borders of Paris in Département Hauts-de-Seine—is the high-rise district known as La Défense, whose urban planning developments began as early as 1955. The Tour Nobel (today Tour Roussel-Hoechst) was the first office tower ever built in France. This 344.4-feet-high building has 31 stories, each with a floor area of 10.700 square feet. The construction is based on a concrete core, which, thanks to the newly discovered slip shuttering of the mid-1960s, could be produced in a relatively short amount of time. The building's floor levels were constructed as lightweight steel floors, each reinforced with 2.6-inches-thick layers of concrete.

The architects responsible for the planning of the building were Jean de Mailly and Jacques Depussé, whose input gave the building its distinctive rounded edges. As the project's freelance supervisor, Jean Prouvé participated in planning and implementing the curtain-wall façade, for which he designed a two-shelled façade. What Prouvé once again attempted here was to secure the panels at every point on the building using the same connecting details. In addition, the rounded edges and two-shelled construction method reduced the possibility of heat loss in the enormous structure. In the event of thermal expansion in the mounting, the panels could slide to an extent and neutralize the incurring tension. To ensure an increased comfort, the façade's closed two-shelled system also allowed Prouvé to ventilate the spaces. Installed in the cavity between the shear walls of the façade, an overpressure regulating system prevented the accumulation of dust.

In recent years the building was rehabilitated by the architectural team of Denis Valode and Jean Pistre. In the process they realized that Prouvé's construction was so simple and well-conceived that the rehabilitation work on the office tower's façade proved to be substantially quicker and less expensive than the work done on the neighboring office towers.

Left page:
The high-rise in the heart of the new housing district of La Défense in the 1970s

1967–1970 ▸ Grid Frame Constructions

Grenoble Fairgrounds, Architecture Department of the University of Nancy ▸ Léon Petroff, engineer

TOTAL gas station, 1969

The altered economic and social situation at the end of the 1960s demanded newer building topologies: what now applied were large constructions with easy to divide ground-floor plans and built using an economical construction method, which, in turn, brought on a change in planning methods, structural calculations, and how constructions were executed.

In the case of the hall for the Grenoble Fairgrounds, which Prouvé completed together with his son, architect Claude Prouvé, the structure is made of a latticework or space frame, which rests on a girder grid; at the same time, the girders are supported by columns called "tabouret" (stools). Evolving from this structure Prouvé developed together with his longtime coworker at C.I.M.T., structural engineer Léon Pétroff, a grid frame construction able to bridge great load-bearing distances.

This system was applied to the 4,186 square yards of the Architecture Department of the University of Nancy, a building dating back to a design by the architects Jacques Binox and Michel Foliasson. Here the net-like framework, produced as a modular system, was arranged diagonally over the building's floor area. With the system he

Architecture department of the University of Nancy under construction, 1970
The support system of the "tabouret" type;
J. Binoux et M. Foliasson, architects

Interior view of the architecture department's art room

Below:
Fairground Hall in Grenoble under construction, 1967–1968
Claude Prouvé, architect

devised, it was the first time that Prouvé succeeded in handling large, load-bearing distances along straight axes (the diagonal being longer than the side of a square's edge). The columns supporting the framework at several points of junction strongly resemble mushrooms with their spreading upper segments. As a reinforcing element, like in the "Alba" construction principle, these also serve the steel and concrete cores, the sanitary blocks for bathroom facilities, and other primary use-related functions. The team working with Prouvé also managed to limit the building's basic structure to no more than five system-related building parts (column, roof, wall, corner connections, and supporting concrete core), which reduced the building costs. Not least of all, the technological aura of the interior spaces conveyed a sober and work-conducive atmosphere in keeping with the building's purpose.

This highly flexible system was also used for a series of gas stations along French highways.

Life and Work

The young Jean with his father Victor Prouvé,
1911

1901 ▶ Jean Prouvé is born April 8 in Paris, the second of seven children to the painter Victor Prouvé and the pianist Marie Duhamel. In the same year, his father co-founds the "School of Nancy".

1916–1919 ▶ Apprenticeship as an artistic blacksmith under Emile Robert in Enghien, near Paris. Beginning 1918 produces his own artistic blacksmith works.

1919–1921 ▶ Continues his studies under Adalbert Szabo in Paris.

1921–1923 ▶ Military service

1924 ▶ Opens his own workshop in Nancy on Rue du Général Custine.

1925 ▶ Prouvé marries Madeleine Schott.

1927 ▶ Meets Pierre Chareau, Le Corbusier, and Robert Mallet-Stevens. Birth of his daughter Françoise.
Entrance portal of Reifenberg's city villa for Mallet-Stevens

1929 ▶ Files first patent on sheet-metal doors. Begins working with the welting of sheet-metal. Birth of his son Claude.
Marbeuf garage for Citroën in Paris

1930 ▶ Jean Prouvé co-founds the modern art association "Union des Artistes Modernes" (U.A.M.). Shows his first furniture and door designs at the U.A.M. exhibitions. Birth of his daughter Simone.

1931 ▶ Restructures firm to joint-stock company "Les Ateliers Jean Prouvé S.A." and relocates to Rue des Jardiniers in Nancy.
Furniture for the Cité Universitaire in Nancy

1932 ▶ Befriends the architects Tony Garnier, Eugène Beaudouin, and Marcel Lods.

1933 ▶ Birth of his daughter Hélène
Study for the omnibus station "La Villette" for Citroën

1934
Standard Chair

Jean Prouvé (at the helm) with his parents and
siblings on vacation in Île Tudy in Brittany

Left page:
Prouvé at the wheel of his Citroën, 1926

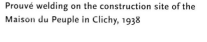
Prouvé and his wife Madeleine

Prouvé welding on the construction site of the Maison du Peuple in Clichy, 1938

Demountable houses for the war injured, commissioned by the Ministry of Reconstruction and Urban Planning.

1947 ▶ Relocation of the workshops to Maxéville near Nancy, and the greatly expanded production of demountable houses and elements, such as walls, doors, and windows. Prouvé employs more than 200 co-workers.

1948
Develops the "coque" system

1948–1951
Meridian Hall of the Paris Observatory (André Rémondet, architect)

1949 ▶ Participation of "Aluminium Français" at the workshops in Maxéville. Prouvé signs a contract with the firm Studal. securing it the exclusive rights to sell the workshops' products.
Begins the works later built in Africa (Algeria and Niger)
Standard houses (Maisons standard métropole) in Meudon (Henri Prouvé, architect)
Maisons tropicales (Tropical Houses) in Niamey, Niger, and in Brazzaville, in the Congo (Henri Prouvé, architect)
"Compas" Table (also dated from 1950–1953)

1950 ▶ Knighted by the legion of honor (Chevalier de Légion d'honneur).
Staircases, furniture, and kitchens for the Unité d'habitation in Marseille (Le Corbusier, architect)
Shed roofs for the Mame Printing Works in Tours.
School Buildings in Vantoux (Henri Prouvé, architect)
"Guéridon" Table (also dated 1949)

1951
Maisons coques (shell houses) for Citroën (design project)
"E.M." table
Façade of the Grand Palais of the Lille Fairgrounds (Paul Herbé and Maurice Louis Gauthier, architects; Désiré Douniaux, engineer)
Develops the "Alba" support system (with Maurice Silvy)

1935
Aero Club "Roland Garros" in Buc near Versailles (Marcel Lods, architect)
Weekend house for B.L.P.S. (Eugène Beaudouin and Marcel Lods, architects)

1935–1939
Maison du Peuple in Clichy (Eugène Beaudouin and Marcel Lods, architects)

1936
Classroom Table with Two Chairs

1937 ▶ Collaborates with Le Corbusier: Develops a model bathroom.
Staircase and garden furniture for the U.A.M. pavilion at the exhibition Exposition internationale des Arts et Techniques in Paris

1939
Demountable barrack units for the French army

1939–1940
Develops the "portique" support system.
Demountable house for S.C.A.L. in Issoire (Charlotte Perriand and Pierre Jeanneret, architects)

1940 ▶ Birth of his daughter Catherine.

1940–1944 ▶ Member of the French Résistance.

1944–1945 ▶ Term of a few months as the mayor of Nancy.

1952 ▶ Prouvé is denied entry to the Maxéville workshop grounds by the stockholding majority of "Aluminium Français".
"Trapez" table
Lecture room chair for the University Aix-Marseille
Four "Maisons coques" in Meudon

1953 ▶ Prouvé resigns from his directorial post and leaves the factory in Maxéville.
Façade of the Apartment Building on Mozart

Live-in trailer, developed together with Pierre Jeanneret, 1939

Jean Prouvé leaning against his 2 CV with his brothers Henri, Pierre, and Victor

Square in Paris (Lionel Mirabeau, architect)

1954 ► Prouvé begins working in Paris for "Aluminium Français".
Prouvé's private residence in Nancy.
Seating for the Cité Universitaire in Antony, near Paris
Pavilion for the Centennial of Aluminum, Paris

1955
Institut Français des Pétroles in Rueil-Malmaison

1956 ► Together with Michel Bataille, Prouvé founds the firm "Les Constructions Jean Prouvé" in Paris.
Pump-Room of the Cachat Spring in Évian (Maurice Novarina, architect)
House for Abbé Pierre in Paris

1957 ► "Les Constructions Jean Prouvé" is taken over by C.I.M.T. with Prouvé as the head of the construction department. Given a chair of "Professionally Applied Art" at the C.N.A.M. (until 1970)
École Nomade (interim school building) in Villejuif (Serge Kétoff, engineer)

Prouvé lecturing at C.N.A.M., circa 1960

1958
Sahara House (prototype)
Develops curtain wall façades for C.I.M.T.

1959
Glass façade and roof additions for Orly Airport South (Henri Vicariot, architect)

1960
Musée des Beaux-Arts "André Malraux" in Le Havre (André Malraux, Raymond Audigier and Guy Lagneau, architects)

1961
Seynave Vaction House in Grimaud (Neil Hutchinson, architect)
Maison Gauthier (Gauthier's House) in Saint-Dié (Baumann and Remondino, architects)
Office building of the firm C.I.M.T. in Aubervilliers, near Paris

1963 ► Receives the Auguste Perret Award of the International Union of Architects.
Develops the "tabouret" support system

1964 ► Exhibition of Jean Prouvé's work at the Musée des Arts Décoratifs in Paris.

1966 ► Jean Prouvé leaves C.I.M.T. and works in Paris as an advisor for design solutions.

1967
Youth center in Ermont

Façade of the Tour Nobel building in La Défense (Jean de Mailly and Jacques Depussé, architects)

1968 ► Begins working on grid frame constructions.
Gas station designs for the firm Total. Fairground hall in Grenoble (Claude Prouvé, architect)

1969
Façade for the Freie Universität Berlin (Georges Candilis, Alexis Josic, and Shadrach Woods, arch.)

1970
Architecture Department of the University of Nancy (Jacques Binoux and Michel Foliasson, architects)

1971 ► President of the jury for the Centre Pompidou Competition in Paris.

1977 ► The Jean Prouvé Exhibition in Geneva.

1980–1981
Radar tower on the Island of Ouessant (J.M. Jacquin, architect).

1981 ► Prouvé receives the Netherlands Erasmus Award. Exhibition of Prouvé's work at the Boymans van Beuningen Museum in Rotterdam.

1982 ► Receives the Grand Architecture Award of the City of Paris.

1984 ► Jean Prouvé dies March 23 in Nancy.

Bibliography

Credits

▶ Allégret, Laurence / Vaudou, Valérie: Jean Prouvé et Paris. Paris: Éditions du Pavillon de l'Arsenal / Picard Éditeur, 2001.

▶ Columbia University, Graduate School of Architecture (ed.): Jean Prouvé: Three Nomadic Structures. Catalog. New York: Columbia Books of Architecture, 2002.

▶ Enjolras / Christian: Jean Prouvé: Les maisons de Meudon 1949-1999. Paris: Éditions de la Villette, 2003.

▶ van Geest, Jan: Möbel / Furniture / Meubles. Cologne: Taschen Verlag, 1991.

▶ Guidot, Raymond / Guiheux, Alain. Jean Prouvé "constructeur". Paris: Éditions du Centre Pompidou, 1990.

▶ Huber, Benedikt / Steinegger, Jean-Claude (ed.): Jean Prouvé. Industrial Architecture. Translated by Alexander Lieven. Zurich: Ed. Artemis, 1971.

▶ Lavalou, Armelle (ed.): Jean Prouvé, Par lui-même (propos recueillis par Armelle Lavalou). Paris: Éditions du Linteau, 2001.

▶ Marrey, Bernard: La „mort" de Jean Prouvé. Paris: Éditions du Linteau, 2005.

▶ Réunion des Musées Nationaux (ed.): Jean Prouvé 1901–1984: Constructeur. Paris: Réunion des Musées Nationaux, 2001.

▶ Rowlands, Penelope: Jean Prouvé. San Francisco: Chronicle Books, 2002.

▶ Sulzer, Peter / Sulzer-Kleinemeier, Erika: Jean Prouvé: Highlights 1917–1944. Basel / Boston / Berlin: Birkhäuser Verlag, 2002.

▶ Peter Sulzer, Jean Prouvé: Meister der Metallumformung. Das neue Blech. Cologne: Verlagsgesellschaft Rudolf Müller, 1991.

▶ Peter Sulzer, Jean Prouvé: Oeuvre complète / Complete works. Vol. 1: 1917–1933, Tübingen / Berlin: Wasmuth Verlag, 1995; Vol. 2: 1934–1944, Tübingen / Berlin: Wasmuth Verlag, 2000; Vol. 3: 1944–1954, Tübingen / Berlin: Wasmuth Verlag, 2004

▶ "architecture", No. 11/12, 1954: 39 above left, 42 left, 43 above, 46 below, 51 left

▶ Archives départementales de Meurthe-et-Moselle, Nancy: 19 below, 23 below, 25 below, 27 below, 28 both, 34 below left, 35 top row, 55 above, 55 below, 61, 67 below, 69 above, 73

▶ © Musée des arts décoratifs, Paris, photo Laurent Sully Jaulmes, all rights reserved: 60 above

▶ Musée nationale d'art moderne – Centre Georges Pompidou – Bibliothèque Kandinsky, Paris: 4, 6, 9, 10 above, 16, 18, 19 above, 20 above, 26, 29, 37 above, 37 below middle, 38, 39 above right, 42 right, 43 below, 46 above, 47 above, 49 above, 50, 51 right, 52, 53 Middle, 53 below, 57 above, 64 right, 65 right, 68, 69 below, 75 both, 79 above, 84, 86, 87 both, 91 Middle

▶ Photo Michel Denancé, Paris: 66, 70 both, 71, 80, 81, 82 both, 83 above, 85 above, 85 below left, 88

▶ "Domus", No. 9, 1950: 44 below

▶ B. Huber, J. C. Steinegger (ed.): Jean Prouvé: Industrial Architecture. Zurich: Ed. Artemis, 1971: 74 below

▶ "L'Architecture d'Aujourdhui", No. 4, 1946: 37 below left

▶ "L'Architecture d'Aujourdhui", No. 1, 1946: 12 above

▶ "L'Architecture d'Aujourdhui", 1964: 15 below

▶ Family Prouvé: 2, 7, 8, 10 below, 11 above, 12 below, 14 both, 15 above, 17, 21 above left, 23 above, 25 above left, 25 above right, 31 both, 32, 34 above, 34 below middle, 34 below right, 35 bottom row, 36, 37 below right, 44 above, 45 both, 47 middle, 47 below, 48, 49 below, 53 above, 54, 55 middle left, 55 middle right, 56, 57 below, 58, 59 above, 62, 63 both, 64 left, 65 left, 67 above, 69 middle, 74 above, 76, 77, 78, 79 below, 83 below, 85 below right, 89, 90, 91 above, 91 below, 92, 93 both, 94 all, 95 both

▶ "La Maison française", July 1957: 13

▶ British Architectural Library (RIBA), London: 24

▶ © Courtesy Galerie Patrick Seguin: 20 below, 21 above right, 21 below, 22 both, 30, 40, 41 below, 59 below, 72

▶ Vitra Design Museum, Weil am Rhein: 11 below, 33, 41 above, 60 below

Quotations p. 7, 8, 9, 10, 12 and 13 from: Huber, Benedikt / Steinegger, Jean-Claude (ed.): Jean Prouvé: Industrial Architecture. Translated by Alexander Lieven. Zurich: Ed. Artemis, 1971.